DIVINE INTERRUPTIONS

DIVINE INTERRUPTIONS

God's Story in the Lives of
Helen & Freddy Johnson

Helen Johnson

ISBN 979-8-218-20940-7

Unless otherwise indicated, all scriptures are taken from *The Holy Bible*,
New Revised Standard Version. Copyright © 1989, 1995. All rights reserved.
Image under Psalm by kjpargeter on Freepik.

Cover art by Ashley Johnson Bell, daughter of the author
(artwithashleybell.com)

Editing & book design by Paul Koning

For Freddy, my soulmate

CONTENTS

If I take the wings of the morning
and settle at the farthest limits of the sea,
even there your hand shall lead me,
and your right hand shall hold me fast.

Psalm 139:9–10

Preface

Chapel Hill, North Carolina

July 2020

"It's been a good ride, Hon."

I had walked into Freddy's room in the intensive care unit moments earlier. Little did I know that I was about to have one of my last conversations with my beloved husband. He smiled his usual peaceful smile as I leaned down and gently placed a kiss on his forehead.

Freddy looked me in the eye, still smiling, and spoke the words that would leave me with the icy certainty that he was going to die.

"It's been a good ride, Hon. We've had a great life together these 66 years. You will not be able to take care of me any longer, and I don't want you to try. I've called hospice, and the ambulance is on its way to take me to their facility in Pittsboro."

"I know," I said, struggling to keep my voice steady. "I know."

The pathways of our lives had been joined for all these amazing years, and I silently prayed that I'd be able to be steadfast beside him in this final decision.

"Promise me one thing," Freddy said, as he held my hand.

"Of course," I said. "What is it?"

"Promise me that you'll write the book—that you'll tell our God-story."

I was numb at this point, holding tight, knowing that I would have to let go as he would soon be transitioning to a life beyond.

"I promise," I whispered.

* * *

Rachel Remen, renowned healer and author, writes: "Everybody is a story. You are a story. I am a story. Our story is about what we faced in order to build what we built… what we drew upon and what we risked to do it… what we felt, thought, feared and discovered through the events of his story in us."[1]

Paula D'Arcy, another author and speaker who's been a friend and guide to me as I've sought to know God more fully, writes: "The journey unfolds as we live it out. My part is to let go with both hands and take the first step. The first step sets everything in motion…. Start walking, the Spirit demands. You are not alone. Love will lead the way."[2]

Everybody is a story. Love will lead the way.

And so, our story—Freddy's story and my story—is about our striving to find that love and about our responding to love's voice. What we heard love's voice asking us from the start was: "Will you follow ME?"

As we intentionally walked the path set out for us and genuinely sought to follow Him, God continued to pose new questions with His divine interruptions. This book relates many such questions and our attempts to answer them. These questions and answers and divine interruptions make up the stories of how God appeared in our lives, spoke to us, and directed our faith journey. They tell the story of Freddy and Helen, yes, but it is truly God's story written on our lives, or—as Freddy called it that July day in his hospital bed—our God-story.

Our Beginnings

F reddy Johnson was born in Raleigh, North Carolina, on January 6, 1940. He grew up in an all-white neighborhood and attended all-white schools until reaching the University of North Carolina at Chapel Hill, an institution that had only been integrated a few years before his arrival. Freddy grew up attending Sunday school and church most Sundays. He was in the youth choir and served as an acolyte at Church of the Good Shepherd, an Episcopal parish in downtown Raleigh. He would later confide that his memory of church was that he never really heard the Gospel. Perhaps his heart and ears were not ready to hear.

I was born Helen Neblett in Richmond, Virginia, on October 30, 1939. My family—mom, dad, and younger sister Jane—moved to Raleigh when I was in the third grade. I attended Sunday school and church at Hayes Barton Baptist Church with my mother and sister while my father played golf. Daddy ended Sunday afternoons on what we called the 19th hole, playing poker and drinking bourbon. Ours was a home of alcoholism and addiction in the days before such things were discussed. Like Freddy, I grew up in an all-white neighborhood and attended all-white schools.

Looking back, I see that my faith journey began with God's questions to my soul. I realize now that it has always been God's questions and His divine interruptions in my comfortable life that challenged me to go deeper into my heart, questions that led me to *seek* and thus to *find*.

I heard the first of God's questions to my soul as a young 13-year-old attending a Baptist summer camp on the North Carolina coast. Under the dark skies filled with sparkling stars, I heard this question: "Do you know how much I love you, Helen? Do you know My deep love for you?"

And in an inexplicable mystery, I responded with all my heart. "I *do* know. I know, and my heart is filled with love for You too!"

As soon as I returned home from camp, I joined my church's youth discipleship group. Not long after joining the group, I was faced with another question: "Am I just believing in Christ, or am I truly following Jesus?" I came to understand that it would be possible to believe while not changing a thing. I knew instinctively that truly following Him would change my whole life! After all, Jesus never said, "Come, acknowledge My existence. I'm the Second Person of the Trinity." But 87 times He said, *"Follow Me."*

As a young teenager, I made the decision to follow Jesus.

Two Become One

As I entered the gleaming hallways of Broughton High School on my first day as a proud member of the class of '58 (the last class to enter as eighth graders), I eagerly checked out all the new faces in the crowded halls as I walked toward my homeroom. I distinctly remember seeing Freddy for the very first time. "That's the cutest guy I've ever seen," I thought as we passed. "Such broad shoulders, and what a sparkling smile! I hope we get to meet!"

Freddy and I did soon meet, and our first date came not long after. His parents drove us to a dance at the Raleigh Country Club. With my bright red hair and my semi-formal emerald green evening dress, I could tell I had captured his heart. We were instantly inseparable. We spent time together most weekends, as Freddy would walk or hitchhike over to my house. We'd play gin-rummy, watch TV in the den, or take a walk to the corner drug store, Johnson's Pharmacy, for ice cream. On Sundays, Freddy would often join us for mother's special beef roast after church.

Before long, Freddy established himself as a halfback on the Broughton football team, and parties at various friends' homes usually followed the games. Hayrides were some of our favorite times, as we snuggled under warm blankets in the hay wagon.

During our junior year in high school, we asked our parents if we could get married, but they told us that they couldn't afford to support us. So we made our own plans to speed the process along.

"I can finish college in three years," I declared. "I think that's the best we can do." And so, with the aid of summer school classes, I managed to push through my program in three years.

Following my graduation from Meredith College, and after a six-year courtship, we set a date for June 23, 1961. Freddy's beloved mother had passed away in February, and partly because of this sad loss, we planned a simple wedding. Even so, my father waged a daily fight against the spending of any money on the plans. Each evening following his fifth of bourbon,

Mom, my sister, and I received his rants about our money issues. A simple wedding would be better for all. My greatest fear, one that consumed my thoughts as we anticipated our long-awaited wedding day, was that my father would not be sober as he walked me down the aisle.

A very small reception was planned at the Raleigh Country Club. Freddy and I stood at the back of the church and shook everyone's hands as friends and family departed the wedding ceremony. Eager for our honeymoon at the Sedgefield Inn in Greensboro to begin, and troubled by my fear of my father's drinking[3], we left the church and hit the road, skipping our own wedding reception!

First Home

O ur first home was a small one-bedroom apartment in Raleigh. With my Art and Home Economics degree from Meredith, I managed to land a job drafting maps with the North Carolina Highway Department. I'd had no training in drafting, only my college classes in Visual Arts Studies. Not knowing the technical names of any drafting tools or equipment, I became the object of much laughter and teasing among the engineers in the drafting department—"Hey, Joe! Pass me that curly thing, please!"

By God's grace, my $200 monthly check covered our rent and provided us with food as Freddy finished his senior year at North Carolina State University. He had begun his college education at UNC-Chapel Hill in geology, but he had soon figured out that engineering would be a better fit. He had transferred to NCSU before his sophomore year to pursue a degree in civil engineering, with a construction option. Along with attending classes, he worked part-time for John Adams, a local builder. At this time, seniors with high grades were excused from exams. Freddy worked hard and was exempt from his exams.

God, We Need You

Our sweet family quickly followed. We had our first child before we celebrated our first anniversary. Keith was born in May of 1962. We have photos of Freddy holding our son while wearing his NCSU graduation gown. Ashley was born in September of 1963, and Kent came along in July of 1964. We were blessed with three babies in 26 months and jokingly said, "Then we found out where they came from!"

Freddy's first job after graduating was as a traveling salesman for Superior Stone Company. His second was with the Cameron-Brown Company, a mortgage brokerage. Soon, however, he joined forces with his best friend, Grady Ferrell, to found their own construction company—Shelter Limited. Grady had business and law covered; Freddy had the construction background.

When Keith was born, we moved from our one-bedroom apartment to a two-bedroom duplex on Medlin Drive. When Ashley was born, we moved again, this time to a three-bedroom triplex on Carolina Avenue. Taking our children to Sunday school and church was important to both of us. With our Episcopal and Baptist backgrounds, we decided to compromise and bring our young children up in the Methodist church. Having made this decision, we joined Edenton Street United Methodist Church in downtown Raleigh.

Kent had been due in September, but he surprised us by arriving on July 29, 1964, five weeks early. As we left Rex Hospital with our tiny newborn preemie, Dr. Winslow, our pediatrician, said, "Call us if he doesn't drink four ounces at feeding times." Those were our only instructions.

Feeding times were not easy or straightforward, but Kent took his four ounces each time, so we made no concerned phone calls to the pediatrician's office. However, at our routine six-week checkup, we received a medical report that would change our lives.

The nurse weighed him, took his vital signs, and left the room. We could tell that discussions were taking place outside the exam room. Then

Dr. Winslow entered and said, as calmly as if he were saying your baby has a common cold, "Mrs. Johnson, your son is in heart failure. We have notified Duke Medical Center in Durham, and they are awaiting his arrival. Is your husband available to take you, or should we call an ambulance?"

In total shock I whispered, "My husband is out of town. Let me call my father first."

Dad was available, and we drove in silence, heavy with the news. An emergency team was waiting for us, and they took my baby away on a cafeteria tray. After a heart catheterization, we learned the devastating news that our youngest son had a complex ventricular septal defect. There weren't surgical instruments small enough to repair such a small infant heart. And so, as we left Kent in the hands of doctors we had just met, a new set of questions arose: "How do we pray, God? For healing? For the impossible? How will we make it? How can we possibly get through this?" These questions caused us for the first time in our marriage to pray—really pray—together. "God, we need the impossible to be made possible. We pray for healing. We pray for Your Presence to be made known to us."

To hear my husband speak simple words of prayer for help broke my heart, but at the same time, it brought unexplainable hope in the change.

A few weeks after the catheterization, the telephone rang in our apartment.

"Mrs. Johnson, this is Dr. Smith from Duke's Pediatric Heart Center. Kent is failing. We would like your permission to do a procedure that is not assured at all but may save his life until the day he can be strong enough to face open-heart surgery. We would place a Teflon band around his pulmonary artery to reduce the force of the blood flow. It's our only hope. Do we have your permission?"

Without waiting for Freddy's input, I immediately responded, "Oh, yes! Please, please do whatever you think might prolong his life."

"We will schedule the procedure for tomorrow at 10. Instructions will be left for you at the receiving desk of the main entrance." I called Freddy immediately and then made arrangements for my parents to take care of Ashley and Keith. It was September 9, Ashley's first birthday. Mother took Ashley to Johnson's Pharmacy to celebrate her first birthday with ice cream at the soda fountain. Oh, how we longed to be two places at the same time, as we missed our baby's birthday.

As Freddy and I drove toward Durham, we became more and more aware of God's presence as we prayed for God's healing hand on our son. Along the road, we passed the Memorial Park Cemetery to the left of the highway. "God, we need Your help once again. By Your mercy, we pray Kent doesn't end up here," Freddy whispered as we slipped past the grave markers in the cemetery.

When we arrived at Duke Medical Center, a nurse guided us into a small cubicle. Dr. Smith soon came in. "As I explained over the phone yesterday, the surgeons will be placing—as a last resort—a Teflon band around Kent's pulmonary artery with the hope of a miracle. We are not sure of the timing, but we will return after the surgery with a report."

"Thank you, Doctor. We are so grateful."

And so we sat, and we waited, and we prayed. Finally, four hours later, Dr. Smith entered the small space and removed his surgical mask. "Well, Johnsons, we think we have seen the miracle we were all hoping for! As the band was tied, Kent's blood pressure dropped into the normal range. Hopefully, this will keep him alive as he grows and adds weight and strength. If all goes well, he will eventually be ready for the open-heart repair he needs. We must be honest, though. The mortality rate is still significant. You will be able to take him home in a few days. We will want to check on him every few months. His lips and extremities will likely turn blue, but that's no cause for concern. We recommend that you treat him as a normal young boy. He's going to make it! You can see him now."

As we walked into Kent's hospital room, we rejoiced. "Thank you, God, for listening and answering our cry for Your help and Your mercy. Our question—God, where are You?—has been answered. We now know that You have always been here with us in this time of fear and worry even when we didn't acknowledge You. Your love has led us through this storm, and we now know that it will be Your love that carries us on the rest of this journey. Thank You! Thank You!"

Mercy Given

As if this period of our lives wasn't stressful enough, we decided to purchase our first home, a split-level with four bedrooms and a full basement for our growing family. It was located on Huckleberry Drive in a new development called Laurel Hills, close to a new elementary school. All this for a grand total of $13,000!

With Freddy's low-paying job, we qualified for Duke's Clinic Care for low-income families. To be of further help with Kent's medical expenses, I began a small craft business supplying a gift shop in the mountains of North Carolina with assorted art accessories for the home—everything from hand-painted lamps, trash cans, and needlepoint canvases to ink thumb prints.

Kent was scheduled every six months for checkups at Duke Clinic. I was an ultra-worried, protective, hovering mom. Freddy was the parent Kent needed. He would throw him in the pool and pitch softballs to him until his lips turned blue. Freddy didn't pamper.

As Kent approached his fifth birthday, the doctors at Duke announced that his oxygen levels were reaching the point that signaled it was time to schedule his corrective surgery. To me, scheduling this risky procedure felt like placing our son under a death sentence. Sadness and worry became my companions once again.

We prayed for the right surgeon for this complicated operation, and we were granted the very best—Dr. David Sabiston, Chief of Surgery at Duke Hospital. (We later learned that Dr. Sabiston rarely operated on children.) God had given us His best.

The date was set. Dr. Winslow, our regular pediatrician, had canceled his office visits in order to watch the four-hour procedure. He assured us that he would report back to us as soon as possible. He was our angel.

I remember Dr. Winslow's smile as he entered the room following the operation. "Well, I have good news! He made it. They are taking him off the heart-lung machine now. But we must wait 48 hours for true results."

On the second day, Freddy went to check on Kent in the recovery room. He was gone for a long, long time. When he finally came back into Kent's hospital room, his face carried a somber expression, lacking his usual smile.

"Well, what's the news?" I asked with trepidation.

My dear husband came over and softly placed his hands on my shoulders.

"Hon, Kent's lungs have collapsed. The doctors have performed an emergency tracheotomy. All we can do is wait and pray." He held me as my knees buckled. I had never before come so close to fainting.

A few minutes later we were asked to leave Kent's room to wait in Duke's large main waiting area. As our beautiful son struggled for life for five long days in intensive care, Freddy and I waited and prayed, waited and prayed. The seriousness of Kent's condition became increasingly evident as we'd pass his medical team in the halls. Some of them would avoid making eye contact with us.

Finally, on day five, Kent's doctors found us in the waiting area and announced the miraculous news for which we had been hoping and praying: "Your son is going to make it!"

As we walked to Kent's hospital room as quickly as we could, tears streamed down our faces. When we reached his side, we covered him in kisses. Our tears were met with his silent cry; no sound came from his lips due to the tracheotomy. Silently I offered praise, "Thank You, God! Thank You for listening and for answering our cries. Our question—God, where are You?—You have answered in the midst of our fear and anxiety! You have been right by our sides and in our hearts the whole time. We know Your great love led the way once again!"

Building Our Lives

Even with the miraculous experience of God's loving presence in our lives during Kent's open-heart surgery, our lives revealed little change. We still sought out and planned our own path of upward mobility and materialism. Co-ownership of Shelter Ltd. had increased our income, and, in our minds, climbing the ladder of success naturally included joining a country club. MacGregor Downs Country Club in Cary had been our choice.

For Freddy, belonging to the club meant hours away from our family playing golf with friends or business contacts. Seeking God's plan for our lives was not yet in our DNA. We had never asked, "God, what were we created for? How might we make a difference in Your world?" I believe a little divine intervention from the Spirit brought the conviction that the money and hours spent at McGregor Downs no longer brought Freddy fulfillment. Over time, he came to better understand the miracle of Kent's recovery and the importance of family. He dropped our membership at the club and used the savings to install a full concrete basketball and tennis court in our backyard for our family to enjoy together.

Even so, our driving motives were still money, success, and the approval of others. Our image was very important to us. Consistent with this desire to move up in the eyes of others, Freddy built us a three-story, 3,600-square-foot dream house on Ridge Road in Raleigh. We were climbing what we saw as the ladder of success by building a more expensive home and leaving the old split-level behind. We bought cars, boats, and a Raleigh Racquet Club membership. We focused exclusively on our family and our home and gave little thought to others. I ran up credit card debt at antique shops and elsewhere in order to make our home presentable to the segment of society we aspired to join. Freddy brought home the latest toys for the children, while I made sure they had the best clothes and—for Ashley—special jewelry. Spiritual development and teaching were not in our toolbox. We left that for Sunday school and church.

Life was good, or so it seemed. Freddy and I both volunteered as youth leaders at Edenton Street United Methodist Church. We saw ourselves as good people performing "good works." We had not discovered what it meant to seek God's guidance for daily living through prayer. We relied on our own ideas and strengths. We valued independence over any kind of dependence on God.

Despite all the outward signs of material success, however, not all was well in our lives. We were overspending and were soon spiraling into debt. Our choice to combat this problem was a move to downsize into a house built by Freddy on Blenheim Drive. We moved from 3,600 square feet to 1,600 square feet. This temporarily helped with our finances, and we lived there for a few years, despite the blow to our egos. But the old itch to design and build our own home resurfaced, and so Freddy built a custom farm-style house just four lots down on the same street. The new home was truly one of a kind, with wood burning stoves and a tin roof—a bit of modern with the traditional. It included a first-floor basement studio equipped with my own pottery wheel and kiln. Ashley was now in middle school, and to encourage her artistic talent, I helped her conduct summer art camps for neighborhood children. Freddy also built a dog kennel in the backyard where we raised three litters of puppies.

In the meantime, Freddy was beginning to experience doubts about the building business. Perfectionist clients were often dissatisfied and negative, causing him great stress. The original joy of building was giving way to a persistent new question: "Is there another, better way for me to make a living?" On top of Freddy's personal situation, the United States was entering the recession of the 1980s. Shelter Ltd. was struggling to provide sustainable income for two growing families.

Looking back, I realize I was close to a nervous breakdown. My life was filled with worry over finances. I was the queen of the people pleasers. "No" was a word foreign to my vocabulary. Ask me to take on a job? There was no question that I could and would do it, even if I knew nothing about the subject. The craziest example was my saying "Yes, sure!" when asked to take on the chairmanship for an upcoming North Carolina Quilt Symposium. I had never made a quilt and wouldn't know where to begin!

To top that off, another "Yes, sure!" came when I accepted the Cultural Arts Chairmanship for Martin Junior High, where our children attended school. I talked the administration into canceling classes for two days for the students to really experience cultural arts. I developed over 75 options in which each student would attend cultural arts classes of their choice over the two days. Typical cultural arts classes like pottery and basket weaving would be offered alongside special classes like Antique Cars and Native American Dance. After numerous persuasive calls on my part to various instructors, everyone was soon on board, donating their time and supplies. I was exhausted and close to a nervous breakdown by the time the event kicked off. While it was successful, and I got the positive recognition that I thought I needed, I was crumbling inside.

Call To Simplify

In the midst of our stressful lives in the early 1980s, I received a phone call from my mother. My father had recently passed away, and she was living by herself. "How would you and Freddy and any of the children like to join me for a weekend getaway at the Blockade Runner in Wrightsville Beach?"

The timing of the offer felt perfect.

"This sounds like just what we need!" I said. "Kent and Keith are tied up, but Ashley, Freddy, and I would love to accept your offer. Thank you!"

A few weeks later, as Freddy, Ashley, and I relaxed on the sand in front of the Blockade Runner Hotel, surrounded by old beach cottages, we began to dream.

"What would it be like to just pack up and move to the beach?" I wondered aloud. "I bet these owners would like to have someone renovate these old beach cottages for them. And, Freddy, I know you would enjoy this laid-back environment. It surely would be a change from building mansions for some dissatisfied customers in Raleigh. No one would know us, and I wouldn't feel the need to fill everyone's requests. A break would be heaven!"

As my vision unfolded, Ashley spoke up. "If you did move down here, I could live with Grandmother back in Raleigh. I could spend my senior year with her. Since she doesn't drive, I could be a big help to her, I bet!"

After some more excited discussion, we left the beach and headed up to join my mother in her hotel room for lunch. When we entered, she looked up from her knitting and asked, "How was the beach?"

"Very interesting," I answered. "And by the way, how would you like to have a roommate named Ashley next year, Mom?"

"Why, sure! Why not?" she immediately responded in her usual positive way.

Freddy looked at me in disbelief. "You're serious!" he exclaimed.

"I'm serious!" I answered with a smile.

Looking back, I wonder if some of our decisions seem abrupt. "Did that really happen?" But I have long believed that God blessed us with a sense that, whenever the Spirit was speaking to our souls, for some amazing reason we knew it, and we would miraculously respond with a "Yes" instead of a "But…" or a "How?" We always moved in the direction of the gift from the voice of love.

And so, that was it! Our lives would take a detour—a divine interruption. We had a new plan. Upon our return to Raleigh, Freddy immediately began the process of stepping away from Shelter Ltd. The idea was simply to move to the beach to "renovate old beach cottages." Within weeks, we put our house on the market. I remained in Raleigh packing up while Freddy and our youngest son, Kent, set out for Wrightsville Beach in search of our next home.

My send-off words to them were: "Just don't make it nice!"

These words came from a heart of letting go of many things including my old mindset of keeping up with the Joneses, the striving to maintain an image of the perfect family and home. It all needed to be thrown in the trash. I was so ready for simpler, smaller, *minimal.* I was ready to put my hands to work. We needed change, and we needed to simplify in order to save our souls. Here was an opportunity for a do-over, and one that would be affordable.

A few days later, I received a telephone call from Wrightsville Beach with Freddy reporting what they had found. "The ad in the paper said it needed lots of TLC, and, Hon, they weren't kidding. It's totally off level, it smells moldy, and there's no heat or air!"

"It sounds perfect!" I responded.

And so, this shack needing "lots of TLC" on Fayetteville Street in Wrightsville Beach became our new home.

Early in August of 1980, we left our home in Raleigh unsold with most of our furniture. As we backed out of our driveway, our minister's wife drove up. She handed us a copy of Richard Foster's book *Freedom of Simplicity.* "I had a nudge from the Lord," she said, "that this book was for you."

As we left Wake County for New Hanover County, I thumbed through the pages and began to read aloud these words from the gift of Foster's book: "Contemporary culture is plagued by the passion to possess.

The unreasoned boast abounds that the good life is found in accumulation, that 'more is better'. We feel strained, hurried, breathless. The complexity of rushing to achieve and accumulate more and more frequently threatens to overwhelm us; it seems there is no escape from the rat race."[4] This book was to be our road map for the next leg of our journey—our spiritual journey. On the way to the beach, we took in our new marching orders.

"Hon, I guess 'less is better,'" Freddy said as he looked across the front seat at me.

"Think we can simplify?" I asked.

"I'm willing!" Freddy answered. "I wonder what our lives will look like as we leave the rat race?"

The artist in me responded, "I visualize a couple strolling along the beach, holding hands, taking in the sunset as a start."

He just smiled.

"It's never too late to heal and start anew. It is not too late because life is this moment, and only this. There is now—this day—and its full potential to open wide a new door. And even though we may tremble at the immediacy and intimacy of the thresholds we face, there is within us the power to walk through these new openings. There is within us a power greater than anything we will ever face, greater than anything we have ever done—a power that enables us to learn from our missteps and begin again." –Paula D'Arcy[5]

Coming Off the Fence

The little white cottage on Fayetteville Street—just two blocks from the ocean—was plain and subtle. It had a small kitchen, a combined living and dining room, two small bedrooms, one full bathroom, and a basement with two more small bedrooms and another tiny bathroom. The basement ceilings were low, only six feet, and the outside needed a new coat of paint. We moved in with a small kitchen table, a few hard chairs, two beds, several lamps, a few linens, and some basic kitchen equipment. The work of getting rid of mold, painting the walls, and leveling the floors was pure joy. Some good friends of ours from high school, Sally and Skellie Hunt, offered Freddy, Kent, and me—along with our dog and cat—a place to stay until the cottage on the beach was livable.

As I took breaks from painting or cleaning each day, I would make space for peaceful walks along the wide beach. These strolls became my time to become reacquainted with Jesus. We began to converse again.

"Lord, thank You for Your sand and sea. Thank You for the peace in me!"

Simple living was grace as we embraced this new concept—the freedom of simplicity!

* * *

Keith was by this time in college at UNC-Chapel Hill. Ashley was living in Raleigh with my mother, just as she had suggested, enjoying her senior year at Broughton High School. Although we planned for her to spend weekends with us at the beach, this didn't happen as often as I had hoped. I felt sad that we were missing so much of her life as a senior in high school.

Kent enrolled at New Hanover High School in Wilmington, not knowing a soul. Living with the Hunts and their two daughters and son was a challenge for Kent, but when we finally moved into our little renovated home at the beach, he was in heaven. Boats, fishing, and surfing filled his days. He even had a man-cave on the ground level of the cottage, complete with a waterbed.

As we continued to work on the cottage at Wrightsville Beach, we renewed old relationships and developed new ones. In September, a new friend, Lyston Peebles, invited Freddy to join him for a Christian men's group at Windy Gap, a retreat center in the mountains of North Carolina.

"If you go and it's not the best thing you have ever experienced, I'll refund your entire retreat fee," said Lyston.

This offer proved sufficiently enticing to Freddy, and it also included an invitation to our friend and former host, Skellie Hunt. Each man thought the other wouldn't actually go, but—miracle upon miracle—when the day came, Lyston picked both up by the roadside where they waited, each ready with a cooler full of beer. The next morning, as the retreat began, an announcement was made: "Would the men responsible for all the empty beer cans please clean them up?"

Once he was over his embarrassment, Freddy settled in to listen to the messages shared during the retreat sessions. The main speaker was the well-known African American evangelist and activist, Tom Skinner.

"As I listened, I became acutely aware of my independent streak and my lack of dependence on the Lord," Freddy shared with me once he returned home. "Tom's message pulled me off the fence I'd straddled all my life. I think being still, surrounded by the beauty of God's creation, among Christian men, I knew it was my time to surrender my life to God—and I did!"

Tears streamed down my cheeks as I reached over with a hug. As we embraced, I realized that my recent gift to Freddy of an easy-to-read Living Bible had not instigated his decision to surrender his life to Christ, but it was constant prayer and God's perfect timing that had brought this good man into God's kingdom.

Soon after his return from Windy Gap, we joined Myrtle Grove Presbyterian Church in Wilmington. Freddy was like a sponge, newly eager to study and learn. He joined a men's prayer breakfast, and we became regular participants in one of the church's small groups. We prayed together regularly as a couple for the first time, genuinely seeking God's will for our lives.

Love Leads the Way

Situated as we were in the middle of a barrier island, it was easy to dream of living directly on the water. Just yards away from our little cottage in one direction lay the sound with its calm waters and its constant parade of passing boats, and not far in the other direction was the ocean itself with its wide beach and rolling waves.

Our pastor at Myrtle Grove, Horace Hilton, and his wife, Tennie, would often invite us to spend evenings overlooking the sound from their pier. One evening as we sat quietly taking in the sunset, Horace spoke up. "You know, the duplex two doors down from this cottage is going on the market very soon. It also comes with a pier that would be perfect for your boat. We'd love to have you as neighbors!"

"We really can't afford it at this time," Freddy said. "I really wish we could. I'd like nothing better!"

But the idea had been planted, and we added it to our wish/prayer list.

A week or so later, my mother called. "I just had another idea. With Ashley living in Chapel Hill now, I'm by myself again. So I'm thinking of moving!"

"Really? Where to, Mom?" I asked.

"I was thinking of Wrightsville Beach! You told me about the duplex near Horace and Tennie. Maybe we could go in together and buy it!"

I was stunned momentarily but quickly recovered. "I'll talk to Freddy about another one of your great ideas, and I'll get back to you soon!"

When I told Freddy about my mother's offer, he said, "This might be perfect—an answer to all our needs. Clara would be close enough to watch over and be with, but we'd be in two separate dwellings."

Like the other detours and divine interruptions along our life's journey, plans quickly fell into place. The duplex was renovated, and mother moved, becoming a resident of Wrightsville Beach. She loved her first-floor space and taking short walks on the beach. She joined a local Baptist church and was soon making new friends. Our larger space on the second floor offered three bedrooms and a larger kitchen than we'd had in the cottage on Fayetteville Street.

* * *

By 1984, Freddy's building business in Wrightsville Beach was struggling. We had discovered that our enthusiasm for renovating old beach cottages was not shared by most beach cottage owners. Most of them simply loved the rustic look. Freddy began to take on some building projects on the more affluent vacation islands of Figure Eight and Bald Head. It was an expensive, unsold spec house on Bald Head Island that was to be the ruin of the business.

This was the year all three of our children were in college simultaneously. I was overcome with worry about paying their tuition and all our other bills. Once again I was determined to work and help pay expenses. Included in our new, larger kitchen was a large commercial convection oven that would cook 18 pies in one firing. Robert's Grocery—a local store in Wrightsville Beach—contracted with me for an assortment of baked goods for the weekend vacationers. I made everything from caramel cakes, corn muffins, croissants, yeast rolls, and chocolate chip cookies to ten different pies. In addition to my baking, I taught bread-baking classes in downtown Wilmington and catered dinner parties on the side. My mother was "volunteered" to clean the fresh crabs we caught for my favorite seafood pasta dish.

These efforts brought little relief to our financial problems. Worry trailed into a deep depression. Not since Kent's heart surgery had I experienced such darkness. Once again, I was a mental mess. There were days, even weeks, during which I didn't get out of bed. Freddy simply didn't know what to do with me. After weeks in this condition, I cried out to God from my pity party. "Where are You, God? This is the pits! I am desperate! We are working as hard as we know how, with little relief. I expected to be blessed as we worked hard to be model Christians, faithfully going to church, studying Your word, praying. Where are You? I don't get it! Please help me trust that You haven't abandoned us. I just don't understand."

In desperation, not knowing where to turn, I grabbed a Bible from the bookshelf headboard of our bed and opened it at random. Looking down at the open Bible in my hands, I was filled with awe as my eyes immediately fell upon these words from the pages of Jeremiah: "For surely I know the plans I have for you, says the Lord, plans for your welfare and not for harm, to give you a future with hope." (Jeremiah 29:11)

"Really, God? Really? This is what You want me to believe? That You have plans for good for our life? To give us a hopeful future? Please help me to trust this word, to know You have not abandoned us. Continue to guide us. Please show us the way. I really don't understand."

Within just a few weeks, God began to reveal his answer to my cry. A group of Christian men—Trip Sizemore, Larry Sitton, Vick Cochran, and Lyston Peebles—who knew of our financial situation called with an invitation. "We would like to invite you to join us for prayer and counsel in Greensboro this coming week. We can meet on Tuesday at Trip and Larry's Law Office. Can you come?"

"Oh my! Thank you. Yes, Helen and I will be there. Thank you so much," Freddy answered.

"Give me a hug," I said, as he put down the phone. "I can feel the heaviness of depression lifting. I can feel a renewed hope in my spirit with possibilities of a potential job offer that would cover tuition and bills." For a moment we just held each other close.

The following Tuesday, we traveled to Greensboro. As soon as everyone had gathered in the law office, Trip opened our time with prayer. Then followed scripture as someone read, "Seek first His kingdom and all these things will be added unto you."

Following the reading, I sarcastically remarked, "Oh yeah. Yes, I remember that verse, a great verse. But what about your advice and wisdom on finding a good-paying job to cover our living expenses and college tuition for three?"

Silence followed with more prayer and more scripture, but no plan. As we drove away, I silently prayed, "Help, God. We need Your help. Please give us the hope we need!"

As we approached Wrightsville Beach and home, God reminded me of the scripture that had been read in the office in Greensboro. I realized then what He was asking of us. "Helen, would you and Freddy seek first My kingdom? That must come first; then all will follow!"

We simply prayed, "God, though we don't fully understand this scripture, we commit to seeking Your kingdom *first*. We trust that You will show us the way."

Within a week, an encouraging phone call came from Greensboro. Trip Sizemore said, "Freddy, we think we have an answer for you. How does a construction job with Hunt Properties sound? You would be helping build apartments in Raleigh."

"Sounds like just what we need. And it sounds like God's answer to our prayer. God's love continues to lead the way."

Miracle Provision

A move to Raleigh for us meant a move for Mother also. We were offered an opportunity to rent a townhome in North Raleigh through Hunt Properties. Mother would move to a newly built condo complex called Parkview Manor, close to her former church in the Hayes Barton neighborhood. She would be near old acquaintances who would provide transportation for her and with whom she enjoyed playing bridge.

The real estate market was sluggish. The "For Sale" sign went up in the yard at the duplex beside the pier. We waited. Finally, a showing was scheduled, and a low bid was received—$45,000 under our asking price.

"There's no way we can accept this," Freddy said. "Where would we come up with $45,000 to pay Clara when we settle at the bank?"

"I don't know either," I responded. "But don't they say that usually the first offer is what you should take? I think we are meant to accept this offer!"

Reluctantly, Freddy accepted the offer, still not knowing where the money would come from. He was also making frequent visits to the chiropractor for a painful stiff neck, another sign of the stress that he was under.

"As we always have, we need to pray, pray, pray," I said. "Lord, we need Your help once again."

And once again, we received a call—another miraculous answer to our plea for help.

"Freddy, this is Dora." Dora was Freddy's stepmother. Freddy's father had remarried several years after the loss of his first wife.

"I'm realizing this house on Harvey Street is too much for me to take care of," she said. "At my age, I need something smaller and maintenance-free. I've made the decision to move to Parkview Manor. Didn't I hear that Clara would be moving to the same place?"

Freddy confirmed that this was true. Dora continued: "Well, I wanted to let you know that in your father's will he stated that when I sell this house and buy something smaller, the difference in the sale prices was to be divided between you and your sister, Kate."

As he put the receiver down, Freddy turned toward me.

"Helen, you will not believe this call. You really won't believe God's provision!" He quickly relayed his conversation with Dora.

"I knew it! I knew it! We serve a mighty God!"

When the house on Harvey Street sold for $189,500 and Dora bought her Parkview Manor condo for $82,500, the difference to be divided between Kate and Freddy was $107,000. We had the $45,000 needed for the closing with mother and a bit to spare!

Becoming Awake

I t's always amazing how God answers our prayers! Always!
In 1984, Freddy and I returned to Raleigh to a new job with Hunt Properties, a rented condo at Whitehall in North Raleigh, and a new church home—Providence Baptist Church. When we joined the church, we became part of a two-year discipleship small group.

As we completed the last study book used by the group, Freddy said what we'd both been thinking.

"Helen, can you believe the path God has taken us down? Growing up at Good Shepherd Episcopal and Hayes Barton Baptist, we never went on mission trips or even really thought about missions. Yet here we are, all these years later, and we're just now hearing about God's heart for mission."

"Yeah," I laughed. "I'm not sure we even knew how to spell the word 'mission' when we started this study!"

"We certainly didn't have a heart for it!" he admitted.

And so, one evening following our study, we prayed: "God, would you give us Your heart for mission? And while you're at it, our hearts are pretty hard at times. Would You break our hearts with the things that break Your heart?"

The same month our discipleship study ended, our pastor—David Horner—announced that a short-term mission trip to Haiti would be available to Providence's members in November of 1986. And so, at 46 years of age, Freddy and I signed up for our first mission trip. In our preparation study before departure, one of the team leaders shared a devotional thought about a time when Jesus asked over and over "What do you want? What do you want Me to do for you?" Someone answered, "I just want to see!" At that moment, my personal heart answer was similar: "Lord, in Haiti I want to see Jesus! I want to see what love really looks like! I believe Haiti is the place. Will You show me?"

* * *

As our plane made its final descent, it was easy to see why Haiti was known as "The Land of Mountains." Rugged terrain stretched as far as we could see. Upon landing in Port-au-Prince, we boarded an old yellow school bus, a relic imported from the United States. As our driver slowly dodged his way through the potholes, we began to take in the sights and sounds and smells around us, many of which we had never encountered before. Crowds of people milled along the streets, simply clad, most with bare feet. Baskets laden with heavy goods were balanced on heads above straight backs. Every time the bus slowed, people reached up to rap on the dusty windows.

"*Blancs! Mwen grangou!*" (Hey, Whites! I'm hungry!)

The smells of burning trash and charcoal filled our nostrils, and the stench of open sewers was unavoidable. Mud huts and dwellings cobbled together out of cardboard and other scrap materials stretched as far as the eye could see. Many of the children showed visible signs of malnutrition, with distended bellies and reddish tints in their hair. Everyone seemed to be selling something—toothpaste, bottled water, bananas, flip-flops—and yet there was no one there to buy. The heat left us drenched. There was no breeze other than the one kicked up by our feeble bus.

After a bone-jarring three hours, we finally reached our destination—Ebenezer Mission. Instantly, the mood changed. A small crowd of people from the compound surrounded the bus. As we climbed down, we were greeted with soft kisses on each cheek.

"*Bonjou! Koman ou ye?*" (Hello! How are you?)

Brilliant smiles radiated from the faces all around us. We were showered with their blessings of hospitality, laughter, and song. The children competed to hold our hands. In that moment and in the days to come, my eyes drank in the love. The children with whom we interacted had no "real" toys, yet they still had real joy. We saw small gestures of touch, moments of caring for one another, the sharing of a simple toy—a wheel made of broken, rusty wire. We watched and learned that among those who possess little, there always seemed to be plenty of time, and a deep trust that even when there are few things to hold onto, there are always many people to love. Each day we were greeted on the dusty paths with "*Bonswa zami mwy!*" (Good afternoon, my friend!). We beheld hope and love. I began to understand that

I was being given a glimpse of Jesus in my Haitian brothers and sisters. God was answering me once again: "This is what love looks like, Helen."

Art Ross, pastor emeritus of White Memorial Presbyterian Church in Raleigh, wrote: "There is a sacred joy in Haiti that defies explanation. The tragedy of the country is evident at every turn; however, many of the people radiate a hope, peace, and joy that is contagious. I have erased any illusion that I can do much to be of help to the country as a whole; however, the gift of friendship seems to be important in the lives of those we touch through our visits. Their friendship and faith have been transformative in my life."

We saw! Love radiated everywhere. We were struck by our Haitian brethren's great needs, yet their lives were filled with so much joy. We were convicted of our own lack of joy amidst such abundance. Might we possibly be intentional in showing God's love to all who came across our path? Might we complain less? Might we learn from their example of offering pure gratitude for the breath and gift of each day? God help us. Spirit of love, enable us to change!

When I think of these eye-opening first days in Haiti, I think of a quote from the author Gernot Candolini, who wrote: "If you haven't grasped it with your hands, you can't comprehend it. If you don't go there with your feet, you can't understand it."[6]

We had sensed God saying, "Come! Come and see! Will you spend time with Me in Haiti? Can you stay awake? Can you look into this day and see beyond the disguise of events and circumstances the shimmering light—the light of Jesus?"

And, once there, we heard "Can you feel the force of love reaching out to you through these Haitian women serving you lunch? This love is the true meal."

Whenever I'm in Haiti I am constantly reminded of certain scriptures that come to life in this atmosphere of less but so much more. In Matthew 14, the story of the abundant feeding of a crowd of five thousand with a mere five loaves and two fish is indeed miraculous. But my friend Paula D'Arcy reminds me that every day we are given five loaves and two fish. This is what we have to work with. Whether or not they are the loaves and fish we intended is outside our control. Whether or not there is a feast is up to us!

As our short-term mission came to a close and we flew back to life in the United States, I recall Freddy saying: "We will certainly come back someday. This was truly a life-giving experience."

Listening to a Nudge

I have found on this journey of following Jesus that God speaks to me in various ways. I have heard Him through scripture, sermons, books, movies, people I encounter, and even road signs. But perhaps the most important nudges to my soul have come through fleeting thoughts.

One morning a few weeks after returning from our trip to Haiti, I sat in my favorite spot on our navy-and-white down sofa in the living room. As I settled in with my bible and journal and a small candle, a thought suddenly crossed my mind with surprising forcefulness and clarity. "You need to sell the Honda!"

"Whoa, God. If this thought comes from You, You're going to have to give this idea to Freddy. Honestly, Freddy has come a long way on this subject—from multiple nice foreign model cars to a simple new Honda. But I'm not the one to make this suggestion. If this thought is from You, You must give the idea to Freddy also!"

The very next Sunday, as we sat at the kitchen table eating lunch after church, Freddy looked up and said, "What would you think of selling the Honda and looking for a used model?"

"Wow!" I exclaimed, hardly believing what I'd heard. "I had the same idea just the other day!"

That same evening, we met with friends from church to play tennis. As we were getting started, we explained to Paul and Macon that we would need to finish early in order to take our car to a used car lot. "We're interested in replacing it with an older car."

"What model is your car?" they asked. "We are looking for a newer model!"

Information was shared, keys were exchanged, and we simply traded cars. We ended up with their used car, and they took over our car payments!

So our Honda never made it to the used car lot. Only later would we come to understand that God was freeing us. We no longer had a house payment, and after the tennis court transaction, we didn't have a car payment either.

Not Now! Not Us!

As I stood in the kitchen with my first cup of coffee, I noticed beside the coffee pot a stack of unopened mail that Freddy had brought in with the newspapers. My eye was drawn to the envelope on top of the pile. It was postmarked Haiti. I put the coffee cup down on the counter, grabbed the letter, and ripped it open.

The letter was from Gabriel Dupree, the Haitian pastor we had visited six weeks earlier. In it, he asked Freddy and me to commit to two years of service at Ebenezer Mission. My eyes couldn't believe what I was reading. I knew in my gut that this letter was God's call. Now. Not 20 years in the future. A Canadian government grant would provide funds for Freddy to build needed churches, schools, and homes. The mission needed a builder. The letter also suggested that I was needed to teach crafts to the local women so that they might start small businesses to help support their families. Notecards, small cross-stitch items such as Christmas ornaments and pin cushions, and other craft items would be sold back in North Carolina at local church bazaars. Also, I would serve as a discipleship trainer for Haitian women leaders.

Standing alone by the kitchen sink, I gripped the counter and thought, "Oh, God, no! I'm going to be sick." I screamed out loud: "No, God! Not now, not us! Don't You remember that we said we wanted to serve You when we retire?"

My head was spinning, and I continued my internal negotiations. We're not particularly brave or courageous. We haven't been to seminary. We really just learned to spell the word "mission." And what about Ashley and Tim's wedding? I began to realize that I had perhaps romanticized my first one-week mission experience. Faced with the reality of an actual call, I knew that I really, really didn't want to leave my family, my kids. How had I imagined that I could endure 110° temperatures, or the sound of voodoo drums, or the scorpions and tarantulas?

"Oh God, please ask someone else, someone more qualified. No, no, no, not us, please! This is impossible!"

As I continued to lean over the sink, I remembered the last scripture I had just written down for my Bible study: "With God nothing is impossible."

In the midst of my panic, in the silence of that very moment, I sensed God whisper to my heart for the second time, 33 years apart, "Do you know how much I love you and Freddy?"

"Yes, Lord, I know so well."

"Then would you come love Me among My children in Haiti?"

Paula writes: "Sometimes there is only the center of God's will and your own 'yes.'"

After catching my breath, I reached for the phone with a shaking hand and called Freddy at the office. With a high-pitched, anxious voice I shouted, "You are not going to believe what just came in the mail!" And I read him the letter.

"Calm down, Helen! You know I'm committed to building the Summit Apartments. This is really, really impossible."

"But... but I just read where Luke says that with God nothing is impossible!"

In his usual calm voice, he simply answered, "Tell you what I'll do. I'll commit to praying together tonight. OK? But this really is impossible."

So that Monday evening our prayer was simple. "God, would You please open and close doors so that we might know *for sure* if this is our call from You."

Two days later, on Wednesday afternoon at 4:00, Freddy called from the office.

"Well, you had better sit down, Hon," he said. "The bank just called and withdrew the finances for the second phase of the Summit Apartments. There's nothing else on the drawing board. It sure seems like this might be one of those doors we prayed about."

In some of our Bible studies through the years, there have been certain scriptures that I would rather omit or not think about. I might even say "This doesn't apply to me." At this critical time in our lives, the scripture God sent our way that we struggled with was Mark 10:29–30. "Jesus said, 'Mark my words, no one who sacrifices house, brothers, sisters, mother, father, children, land—whatever—because of me and the Message will lose out. They'll get it all back, but multiplied many times in homes, brothers, sisters, mothers, children and land…."' (*The Message*)

But this was His word for Helen and Freddy at that moment, to leave our family, our children, our lifelong friends, to go and love Him among the children of Haiti.

Our adult children were by this time living away from home. Keith was in law school at the University of Virginia in Charlottesville. Ashley was teaching art in Statesville, North Carolina. And Kent was attending N.C. State University in Raleigh. We would gather as a family only on holidays and some special weekends. So, to announce these radical plans around the dining room table was not going to be possible. The message regarding our plans was delivered by phone—certainly not the best way. Two of our children expressed sadness about our leaving.

For the third time in my 46 years, I entered a state of deep depression. Our bed became my home for the next month. Freddy brought me meals on trays. I was stuck living in a dark place of sadness. In this desperate state, I remember offering a simple prayer: "God, help me. The only way I can do this is if You will change the hearts of our children. That's the only way we can answer Your call to Haiti—the *only* way."

Within a few weeks following my desperate prayer, Pastor Gabriel came to Raleigh and spoke at our church. He closed the evening with powerful, heart-wrenching stories of life in Haiti, and he reiterated the need for us, Helen and Freddy, to come and help God's children and our neighbors in Haiti. Pastor Gabriel ended his talk by announcing that Ebenezer Mission had received a 7-to-1 matching grant from Canada.

"With this blessing, Ebenezer needs Freddy to help us build houses, school, churches. And I hope Helen will use her art talent to teach and develop a craft business for the women at Ebenezer, as well as offer discipleship training for the women in the community. We would welcome your financial help toward this grant from Canada. We thank Providence Church for sending this couple to serve with us."

Straw baskets were passed along the rows of the congregation. Approximately $15,000 was raised that night, with the promise of over $100,000 to be given for building projects through the matching grant.

Following the service, Pastor Gabriel met with our children and my mother in a conference room at Providence, further explaining our call. Following the meeting, our family came to us and said, "You have no choice. You *must* go." We received their blessing with gratitude, knowing that they too were making a sacrifice—letting go.

Looking back, I can see clearly that the invitation to join God in Haiti was a turning point. Accepting that invitation would move us from studying God as an Object to knowing and experiencing Him as a Subject who would totally change the way we would experience our lives from that point forward.

Provision for God's Plan

In the midst of the crazy month of January 1987, our friends Mildred and C.A. Dillon called with a generous offer. They had heard about our plans to move to Haiti, and they wanted to help.

"What are your housing plans during this transition?" they asked. "We wanted you to know that we have a full basement apartment, and we would love for this to be your home as you work toward leaving for Haiti."

We immediately accepted this amazing offer. We gave up our rented condo in North Raleigh and moved into the spacious basement apartment in the Five Points neighborhood of Raleigh. Our days were filled with planning for Ashley's wedding, which was scheduled for June 20, 1987. Our furniture and other belongings were divided among our children. We began to fill an old diesel Suburban that we planned to ship to Haiti. We packed it with family photos, my favorite blue linen napkins, devotional books, Bibles, some clothes, lavender-scented candles, a favorite antique basket, hygiene items, toilet paper, and anything else we thought might prove useful in Haiti.

As we continued to plan and pack, we gathered together a group of men and women to serve as a support team, to help raise financial support, certainly, but most importantly to support our ministry through prayer. One of the challenging moments of meeting with people during this time came when two of these friends challenged us *and* God's call: "I don't believe God would call you to leave your family. You are not being responsible as a Christian father, Freddy. I want no part of this."

So, we realized, following Jesus would mean losing friends. One member of our support team, Robert Boone, asked after our two friends left, "How are you doing with this right now, Helen?"

I answered with a strong voice, "I know that I know in my spirit that God has called us. I regret that we can't get everyone's approval, and I'm sad to lose these relationships, but the most important is our relationship with the Lord. I have to do what I have to do. I just know we have to do it. Some friends don't understand and criticize us but I know the Word planted in my heart at this time!"

"Well, I recommend that you take another short trip to Haiti. I think a quick revisit to Ebenezer would be wise before you go down permanently."

Freddy thought this was a good idea, so a quick three-day weekend trip was arranged for the first of February. The purpose was to better understand our call—where we'd live, what we were to do, and what we might bring with us. Pastor Gabriel met us at the airport that Friday in February and began filling us in as we drove the potholed stretch from Port-au-Prince to the Ebenezer compound in Gonaives. He once again explained the plans for multiple building projects that Freddy would undertake. He also laid out plans for me to study Haitian Creole with Elda before teaching crafts and doing discipleship training with the women of Ebenezer Mission.

The next day, we walked across the road beside Ebenezer Mission and out onto the flat, dry plot of land behind the hospital. Pastor Gabriel said, "This is the piece of land where a duplex will be built for your housing."

Standing on the hot sand, we looked out across the flat plains to the mountains in the distance, under the azure blue sky. "Can't you just picture us looking out from our kitchen window over this peaceful, gorgeous view?" I asked Freddy.

"Yes, I can imagine it. And an even better thought is having our children visit and having a meal together with our new Haitian friends. I can only imagine!"

"Yes, we can do this!" I thought, trying to remain positive.

On Sunday we attended church with the other missionaries and Haitian families who lived within the compound. A translator interpreted the sermon from Creole into English for us. As we left in the late afternoon to drive back to Port-au-Prince, our eyes beheld our Haitian brothers and sisters walking along the roads just as we had on our initial visit, but our hearts carried a new prayer.

"Lord, give us Your love for our new neighbors. May we serve them— and You—in our new home here. We need Your love to lead the way!"

This Is For Sure

Upon returning to our new temporary home with the Dillons in Raleigh, we began to work more earnestly on the task of seeking "faith support," a new phrase in our vocabulary. Raising such support means sharing your call from God with friends, family, and any other interested people and asking for financial support to meet the budget requirements for one's anticipated ministry. Plans were set for donations to be mailed to Providence Baptist Church so that any gifts would be tax deductible. Support-raising was a humbling experience for Freddy, who had always held salaried jobs and was used to giving to nonprofit organizations. He now stood in an uncomfortable new position—asking for money!

Still in the mode of testing God, we prayed, "God, this call *still* seems impossible. To be sure, to be really sure, this is Your call, we pray that the total of the budget will be reached by March 15, 1987. If the target is not reached by that date, we'll assume this is not our time—yet!"

But once again God was not to be deterred. I remember well the day before the March 15 deadline. We were still $5,000 short of the budget. I was having a major meltdown in the quiet of the basement apartment, with tears and angry shouts. "God, this walking by faith is the pits—really the pits! Are we to be seen as fools? We have hardly any belongings, and now what? I really don't understand. We were so sure this was your call!"

My cries were interrupted by the sound of the phone ringing in the dim light of the basement apartment. I picked up the receiver and heard the secretary of Providence Baptist Church say, "Helen, I know I don't usually call, but I thought you'd want to know. A check for $5,000 just came in from your friend Tommy Drake."

I sank to my knees in awe. This was *for sure*! Just another one of God's many miracles.

Celebrating Love

W hat does a wedding provided by missionary parents look like? Picture if you will a village of dear friends and family offering gifts galore to fill every need.

For Freddy and me, the many wedding provisions began with our best friends, Bob and Maggie Wynne. Bob was president of both Brown-Wynne Funeral Home and Fallon's Flowers, two local Raleigh businesses.

"You could have Ashley and Tim's reception here in our home and yard on Holt Drive," Bob offered. "Folks could easily walk the three short blocks from Hayes Barton Baptist Church to our house. They could even park at the church parking lot! We'll provide the bouquets for the bride and bridesmaids from Fallon's and a Brown-Wynne tent for the reception in the backyard!"

During the time prior to the wedding and while we were preparing for Haiti, I had taken a part-time job sewing, of all things, bridal veils to make a little extra cash. The shop owner generously made Ashley's beautiful veil as a gift. Her lovely wedding dress was purchased on sale at Montaldo's.

On the day of the ceremony, EsDorn Westbrook—a flower designer from Fallon's and a dear friend—created a lovely arbor of greenery and flowers at the altar of the church, perfectly setting the scene for the love that would be spoken by Ashley and Tim to one another and the love that would be offered to us all by friends on that special day.

As the nine bridesmaids surrounded the couple, their arms were laden with beautiful pastel bouquets, gifts from Fallon's Flowers. Our friend and pastor, Horace Hilton, and my minister uncle from Virginia, Charles Watkins, officiated the wedding ceremony.

Following the ceremony, all the guests left the sanctuary and strolled along the sidewalks of the Five Points neighborhood to the home of Bob and Maggie on Holt Drive. We were greeted with classical melodies from a harpist nestled among the ivy vines on their front lawn. Flowers from Fallon's cascaded down the banister of the interior stairway and adorned every table in the beautiful Victorian home. Among the covered dish offerings brought by friends, the silver trays piled with sliced prime beef on homemade yeast rolls proved to be a favorite.

The borrowed funeral tent from Brown-Wynne (with the business name on the tent artfully concealed by hanging ivy) provided shade but little relief from the June heat.

"We better cut the cake soon," I mentioned to my friend Mildred Dillon. "It's starting to look like the Leaning Tower of Pisa!"

With God's provisions and the generosity of so many friends, the entire wedding—probably worth $15,000 or more—was put together for less than $1,000.

New Roommates—Rats and Scorpions!

Within two weeks following Ashley and Tim's wedding, we were set to depart for our new home—Ebenezer Mission in Gonaives, Haiti. Events did not, however, unfold according to our plans. We received word that due to political unrest in Haiti, our flight scheduled to leave for Port-au-Prince on the first of July had been canceled.

"This isn't a very good sign, Hon," I said. "I'm feeling a bit anxious!"

"I think it's time for us to do a bit more research," Freddy answered. "Let's spend some time tracing the history and see if we can better understand what's going on."

At this point, we'd had no language study and no cross-cultural training of any kind. Our knowledge of the political situation in Haiti was sketchy, at best. All we had was the Divine voice of love inviting us to join Him in Haiti. Becoming better informed suddenly felt like a good idea.

As we read, we learned a great deal about the political turbulence we were about to enter. Less than two years earlier, Haiti's notorious dictator Jean-Claude "Baby Doc" Duvalier had been forced to flee after 15 years in power. During his corrupt rule, he and his family had lived lavishly while his country had languished as one of the least developed nations in the western hemisphere. Thousands of Haitians were tortured, killed, or exiled under the Duvalier regime, while the remainder lived in abject poverty.

After Duvalier's ouster, a National Governing Council under a military general was established to administer the government during a transitional period that would ostensibly lead to democratic elections. During the months that followed, tensions continued to build. Soldiers and other paramilitary groups dominated the streets; roadblocks were ubiquitous. We were due to arrive as violence, chaos, and uncertainty pervaded the country.

Our flight was eventually rescheduled for mid-July. As we boarded the plane after saying our goodbyes, I heard the Divine whisper once again: "Have no fear. I am with you."

After a stopover in Miami, we flew onward to Port-au-Prince. As the wheels of our American Airlines jet touched down on Haitian soil, I looked out the window toward the barren mountains. I took a deep breath and, with my hand over my heart, said, "We are home, Hon!"

The tiny airport was chaotic. We collected our few pieces of luggage, passed through customs, and began to look around. Amongst the crowds of people massed outside the airport doors we spotted Pere, a member of the Ebenezer community, waving to get our attention. He directed us to a small jeep, and we pushed toward it through the people, many of whom stretched out their hands, begging the new arrivals for a dollar.

We loaded the jeep and set out for Ebenezer Mission. As Pere dodged the deep potholes on the now-familiar three-hour trip, our minds had time to look ahead. I thought again of our hopes and dreams for a new life of service among God's children who were living on the margins. I thought of the promised duplex, our new home in Haiti. I envisioned the breathtaking views of the mountains in the distance. I dreamed of using my gift of hospitality, adorning our dining table with my favorite blue linen napkins as family came and Haitian friends gathered around our table. I could see Freddy in his "happy place," constructing homes and schools and churches, fulfilling his passion to provide for those in need. And I was excited about learning Creole, teaching amazing art lessons, and leading discipleship training for the women of the local church. We were both pumped!

When we finally arrived at the Ebenezer compound, we soon learned that all we had envisioned, dreamed about, and prayed for was not to be.

No duplex stood on the dusty plot we'd been shown. There wasn't a kitchen window from which to gaze out at the mountain views. And worse, there were no funds for Freddy's building projects. The Canadian government grant had been withdrawn.

We stood facing Pastor Gabriel on the bare, hard-packed earth in front of the cinder block facade of the existing elementary school. We were stunned by what we were hearing.

"Oh, I am sorry," Gabriel muttered, his usual charisma gone. "We don't know why the Canadians have withdrawn their grant, but because of this we haven't had the funds to build your home."

He pointed up at the second floor of the school building. "For the time being, you will stay in that room on the second floor of the school."

Our hearts sank further when we learned that all of the mission's building equipment and tools were in storage behind a securely locked door and the only key was in the pocket of Mike Corby, a missionary who was on leave in the United States. Freddy had no funds for building and no equipment with which to build.

Gabriel also informed us that my designated Creole teacher, Elda, had been sent to the United States, so there would be no Creole lessons, no art lessons, no discipleship training.

We carried our few pieces of luggage up the stairs to the room that was to be our temporary home. We stood in disbelief.

The doorway had no actual door; only a piece of cloth hanging from the frame offered privacy. Like the school below, the single small room's walls were of rough cinder blocks. A single bare lightbulb was suspended from the ceiling by an extension cord. The only furnishings we saw were a table, a single wooden straight-back chair, and a double mattress. The room had no windows, though there was a small gap between the cinder block walls and the frame of the tin roof. We would soon learn that the gap was an open invitation to mosquitoes, scorpions, and large rats, our nightly companions.

I crossed this new threshold and made my way over to sit on the mattress. I ran my fingers across the thin coverlet stretched over the bed. As I sat, I remembered a quote from Paula D'Arcy: "Thresholds demand a willingness to walk in new directions. They ask us to 'not know'—we who are so in love with knowing. They insist that we be led where we never intended to go. They will not respect the hunger that feeds the ego and keeps us small. They speak of a LOVE far different from the one we know."[7] Could I trust that this new threshold would bring me to a deeper knowledge of a LOVE I had not known?

A fine black silt from the surrounding desert coated everything in the small, barren room. I was reminded of a Haitian proverb given to us as we departed the United States: "If there is anything you need and don't see, please let us know, and we will show you how to do without it." Wow! What a prophetic word that was turning out to be.

"At least there's a tin roof and a cement floor," I tried to convince myself. After all, we had a mattress and two flat pillows, while outside these cinder block walls families were surviving in mud huts with straw roofs and mere mats to sleep on. We had an army trunk for our clothing, while our neighbors' means of storage might be a single nail in the mud wall for their single change of clothing. We had learned during our earlier visits that larger families sometimes had to sleep in shifts, and pupils would crowd under the single streetlight outside the walls of the mission compound to read their studies and do their homework.

The first night, I was awakened by the unfamiliar noises of the dark tropical night. I sat up in bed and frantically punched Freddy on the shoulder.

"Listen! Do you hear firecrackers in the distance?" I gasped.

Yawning and softly patting my arm, he said, "Hon, try to go back to sleep. I'm afraid that's gunfire from Gonaives and not firecrackers we hear. We'll be OK. Now try to sleep!"

During another early night, as we lay awake enjoying bands of moonlight streaming in through the opening beneath the roof, I heard Freddy say softly, "Don't freak out, Hon, but I think I just saw a huge rat racing along the extension cord above our bed!"

I grabbed his chest and snuggled close, before peeking up toward the ceiling. Sure enough, we had a new roommate—a foot-long rat!

A few nights later, my sleep was disturbed as I sensed something crawling across my shoulder as I lay on my stomach. With a single convulsive swat, I knocked whatever it was from my body. I reached for a flashlight on the floor beside the bed and clicked it on to discover that the culprit was a now-dead scorpion!

"Most steps toward greater openness and awareness are preceded by a certain amount of fear and risk. The road ahead cannot be fully predicted in advance and no ultimate security can be found in the end. If we are to move forward, we move ahead in spite of fear and not because we have none." –Paula D'Arcy

I Am With You

"Why did You call us here, Lord?"

This became for Freddy and me a daily question.

One day I sat alone in our dark room in a deep depression. "Lord, none of the plans we thought You had for us have materialized. We were so *sure* You called us to love You here. But not a single house has been built. We haven't learned the language. I am so lonely, Lord. I miss my children. Please, please help us understand. *Help!*"

As I sat at the edge of the mattress, head in my hands, wiping the flood of tears from my cheeks, suddenly the fabric hanging across the doorway was pushed aside. A lovely young Haitian girl stepped across the threshold. She smiled at me and then began to sing in English: "God is so good. God is so good. He's so good to me!" When the song was finished, she backed out of the room.

In the awe of the moment, I was overcome by the presence of God with me. I sensed a voice to my heart: "I *am* here with you. You are not alone. I *am* with you! I will *always* be with you. And I am with your children at home!"

As I was lonely, I came to know, Lord, You were lonely;
As we were persecuted, I came to know, Lord, You experienced this even greater;
When we lost friends who thought we were irresponsible,
When we lived in poverty,
When our hearts were broken,
I knew You knew loss... poverty... abandonment.
Oh, how Your heart must have been broken!

Because of what I was going through, it dawned on me what a privilege it was to experience things similar to those Christ himself had known. And so I resolved that, going forward, whenever the hard places come—and they will come—my question will be "How did *You* experience this, Lord?

Daily Life

Freddy was introduced to the construction workers at the mission—Pere, Majuste, Saint Pierre, and Jean Claude—and he would join them for small jobs around the compound. He soon developed strong relationships with several of the men. Years later, Pere said, "Freddy was like a father to us. We learned a lot about building and construction as he shared his wisdom with us. We were like brothers. He had such a giving heart. Noticing the open-toe sandals that we worked in, he arranged for fine leather work boots with laces to be sent from the USA for all of us!" (These boots were donated by our friend Monty Mantey, owner of Shoe Shack in Wilmington, NC.)

As Freddy made himself as useful as possible, I continued to struggle. I had been told that I could expect to be able to make telephone calls to the States from the Bell South Office a few miles away in Gonaives. I was counting on this small luxury. After all, if I was going to leave my children behind to follow Jesus to Haiti, the least I could expect was a weekly call home. What deep sorrow it was to learn that the international lines were down due to the ongoing violence and unrest.

"I guess this means we won't be able to hear the sweet voices of our children," I said to Freddy in disbelief. Regular communication with our family was not to be.

Freddy and I had also imagined that our two-year stay would include visits from our children. As it turned out, Keith, our oldest son, now a law student, was the only one to make the trip.

On the day he arrived, Pastor Gabriel immediately said, "Keith, I need your legal advice for some business in Port-au-Prince. Would you go with me in the early morning tomorrow? We'll need to get going at about 5 a.m.!"

So Keith and Pastor Gabriel set out before dawn for the capital city. They returned at dusk. Keith shared with us how the day had gone.

"When we were about halfway to Port, we came across a horrible wreck. The brakes of a large, overloaded truck had given out."

With no brakes, the open-backed *kamyon* had barreled at high speed up and over a tall embankment. The crash had left the truck's cargo of men, women, and children, and all their goods destined for market—charcoal, bananas, even goats—strewn across the hillside and the highway.

"It looked like a bomb had gone off!" said Keith. "As we pulled up, a Haitian man was standing in the road waving his arms frantically, pleading for us to stop. Pastor Gabriel rolled down his window and began talking to the man in Creole. In the background I could hear the bleating of injured goats and the moans of the human passengers. I kept hearing Gabriel say '*Pa, pa; non, non,*' and then suddenly we drove off! We left without helping a soul!"

When Keith had asked why they hadn't stopped to help, Gabriel had explained that in Haiti, when you take anyone to the hospital, you become responsible for that individual's care and must bear the cost of that care. "So, no one can afford to help," he said.

"Dad, it was the worst thing I've ever seen."

* * *

Soon after Keith returned to the States, two of the missionaries at Ebenezer—Peggy McCracken and Taz Fields—left to go on furlough. Their small two-bedroom house was made available for our use. We had real doors and screens in the windows and a shower! Directly across the yard stood another small house shared by two young men, our new neighbors. One was Stan Wiebe, a Canadian with an accounting background who had committed to serve for two years. He was developing accounting systems for Ebenezer Programs and training nationals in accounting. Stan's roommate was a very tall, skinny Belgian named Alain Lescart. Alain taught and discipled the students in the high school. My new job became, as Alain described it, "to take care of our bodies!"

Because we were without refrigeration of any kind, I made almost daily trips by jeep to the local street market for fresh fruit, vegetables, rice, beans, cheese, and bread. These were the mainstays of our dinners. My home economics training was paying off.

"Stan, could you help us get some chicken?" I asked one day. "I'd love to add some protein to our daily rice!"

"Sure, I'll try!" he said. Stan was the only one in our little group who could speak some Creole.

Later that day, I heard a knock on the door. When I opened it with curiosity, I beheld a young Haitian girl with her hands extended toward me. In them she held a squawking, white-feathered chicken, very much alive.

"*Bonswa, madam! Pou ou!* (Good afternoon, madam! For you!)" she smiled.

"Oh! *Pa, pa* (No, no)," I answered. "*Mèsi anpil* (Thank you very much) but, oh my, I can't kill a chicken, or pluck its body!" I would have to take care of Stan, Alain, and Freddy's bodies in another way!

Saved By an Angel

One part of our job responsibilities at Ebenezer was to facilitate the in-country activities for groups coming to Haiti for short-term mission experiences. However, with the escalating violence and unrest, fewer airlines were flying in, and thus fewer teams were coming.

What turned out to be the last scheduled mission trip was a group from our own Providence Baptist Church in Raleigh. Our week with the team was spent hearing testimonies from our Haitian friends, offering hands-on help at the hospital, and conducting a vacation Bible school for Haitian children from the local community. On the team's last day, we planned to tour several neighboring villages in Ebenezer's open-backed truck. Little did we know that God had a miracle in store for us!

As we all piled into the bed of the truck to leave Ebenezer, I reminded everyone to check for their water jugs, sunscreen, and hats. We were anticipating a long, hot day.

When we approached the nearby village of Lestaire, we saw a roadblock ahead. Stretched across the highway were stacks of old rubber tires, planks of wood, and broken metal poles. The truck ground slowly to a halt. The roadblock was flanked on either side by soldiers in khaki garb, rifles hanging casually from their shoulders.

"*Agoch, agoch!* (To the left, to the left!)" one of the soldiers shouted to our driver. Turning left meant taking a detour down a rough and rutted track into the heart of Lestaire.

Having no real choice, our driver steered the heavy vehicle onto the track and began picking his way down the slope as we all hung on as best we could. Suddenly, the driver slammed on the brakes. Fear gripped our souls as we realized that a second roadblock lay across the mud track dead ahead. We were trapped between the two. In a matter of moments, the truck was surrounded by shouting men. We could see that several of them were picking up stones. All around us we heard the angry chant: "*Blanc! Blanc!* (White! White!)"

Deeply aware of our role as leaders of the group, Freddy and I tried to remain calm. We had no phone, and we knew there was no hope of help from the police or U.S. authorities. Several of the men started to climb up the sides of the truck, stones in hand. Who can explain the pain and anger we saw in their faces? It seemed we were moments from being stoned!

Freddy shouted, "Alright everyone, our only hope is to pray. Pray like you never have before!" And so, in unity, our desperate voices rang out: "God of mercy! *Help us!*"

And then, a miracle—a for-real miracle. Just as we thought we might be facing death, from out of nowhere a young Haitian man appeared in front of the truck. As he approached, he began to speak loudly.

"*Bonjour!* My name is Daniel," he said in English. "I am attending the Bible college over the hill. I greet you in the name of the Lord!"

The rest of his words were a blur; I really have no idea what he said to us or to the men. All I remember is that the angry voices fell silent, and the men all climbed down off the sides of the truck. They cleared the tires and other debris from the track and opened a way to freedom. God had shown us mercy at our time of greatest need. We were saved!

Was the Bible student an angel sent in answer to our prayers? I'm not sure. What registered in my heart was that God had provided His mighty protection. And I became more aware than ever that I could always count on Him, trust Him, no matter the situation.

Lessons Learned

Within weeks of our arrival in Haiti we had become acutely aware of deep differences between the ministry vision of Pastor Gabriel and our own vision. In our earlier interactions, especially during his fundraising trip to North Carolina, he had been charismatic and inspirational in describing the needs of his constituents and his far-reaching plans to meet those needs. We and the other members of Providence had eagerly bought into his enthusiasm. We all felt called to help our brothers and sisters in Haiti in any way that we could.

However, once we were on the ground, immersed in the daily life of Ebenezer, we began to see a different side of the ministry's leader. There seemed to be little follow-through on the many plans he had described. A number of projects that had been started had seemingly been set aside. The school and clinic were ill-equipped. Other buildings stood half-finished. And, of course, our promised house had never even been started. Gabriel always seemed to be working on the next big idea for which he would need outside funds, but we were now seeing all the previous big ideas in various states of neglect.

As newly arrived outsiders with little previous cross-cultural experience, we didn't feel it was our place to be critical of the way the mission was run, but we also wanted to be good stewards of our time and of the resources our supporters back home had freely given to send us. Our hearts felt an increasing sense of unease. It didn't help matters to learn that Gabriel had been heard referring to us as "two big fish." Did he see us only as a source of cash?

We expressed our feelings to a few key supporters back in the States. One wrote: "I'm reminded to pray for lasting progress in the development of the Haitian mind and heart, which is not meant to be Western development, but that which develops them into the full plan for all of creation as seen by our God as He looks down on Ebenezer."

Freddy and I felt this keenly. We truly wanted Gabriel to succeed and the mission to be fruitful. We certainly had no desire to step on cultural toes, but we also had to wrestle with the discomfort we were feeling about the lack of accountability we were seeing. The thought of confronting Gabriel filled me with dread.

Again we received encouragement in a supporter's letter: "I try to force myself to pray about the differences in approach to life which are cultural, especially in regards to planning, communication, and accountability. I realize there exist honest differences, and I hope and pray to understand them better. However, Ebenezer has to understand that U.S. Christian involvement is not a rubber stamp. All that Gabriel wants to do is not profitable. If he thinks God has called the folks we associate with to be involved, he is going to have to become more accountable to them, especially in the area of planning and accomplishing plans."

The same letter suggested that being pushed to confront Gabriel against our natural tendencies might actually be an opportunity for our own growth in Christ. Whoa. These words would come to seem prophetic in later years.

We finally reached a breaking point when Gabriel revealed his latest idea. He had decided that what Ebenezer needed was a university. He was already talking about raising funds for the project in the United States. We knew then that we could stay silent no longer.

Our leadership at Providence assured us that they were behind us: "You should not feel the need to bear this by yourselves." We let the other missionaries in the compound know of our plans to confront Gabriel. Both Peggy and Taz offered to accompany us, but we decided it would seem less threatening if we went on our own.

When the time came for the meeting, we soon realized he had received advance warning. We laid out our concerns as gently and respectfully as we knew how, but he had quick, defensive answers to most of our points. When I shared my lament that the original plans for our ministry had failed to materialize, he blamed it on the withdrawal of the grant. When Freddy raised his concerns about all the unfinished projects, he listed all the urgent needs that had diverted his attention and the limited funds available. When we asked about the nice house that had been built for his mother-in-law, he said that

Haitians look at how you treat your family and that he had been embarrassed of the mud hut in which she had been living. We didn't get a clear answer about how it had been paid for.

We assured him of our love for him and for the people served by Ebenezer. We praised his gift of pastoring and told him that we believed him to be sincere. But we were also very clear about our conviction that the ministry needed greater accountability, especially in the area of finances, and that we could not in good conscience continue to be involved without assurances that these concerns would be addressed.

"We are concerned for the downfall of Ebenezer," Freddy said. "We think the university will be the straw that breaks the camel's back. By staying, we would be perpetuating what we sense to be wrong."

Again, Gabriel responded defensively. He made it clear that if we could not support him fully, he did not want us there.

We grieved the breaking of our relationship, but we felt sure we had done what we had to do. Much time would pass before we would fully understand what God was teaching us, but at the time it was enough to simply obey.[8]

Real Call Revealed

B y November of 1987, we knew that God was releasing us from our two-year commitment. The first attempt at free elections had been scheduled for November 29, but the country was in turmoil during the runup to the vote. Riots were a daily occurrence. Buildings burned—the streets were utter chaos. The sound of gunfire rang through every village. We heard reports of multiple killings by machete and by bullet. Government buildings were all closed. Only a few flights were coming into or leaving Haiti. We booked seats on one of the few departing flights.

I remembered the scripture from Jeremiah that God had given me three years earlier in Wrightsville Beach, during my depression. "For I know the plans I have for you, Helen. Plans for good. Not for evil. Plans to give you hope and a future." I trusted God's word that the plans He had for us would be to give us hope and a future. We held His promise in our hearts.

Two days before Thanksgiving, we made our move. We kept hearing of canceled flights; we could only pray that ours would not be one of them. We had no way to communicate, so we just had to head for the capital city and take our chances. Looking back, I think I was in a state of shock as we fled the chaos. Most of what took place is a blur.

We made the three-hour journey to Port-au-Prince without interference. Our destination in the city was Wall's International Guest House, a place we had stayed before. We arrived safely, but as we settled into our room and started checking our documents, Freddy exclaimed, "Oh, no! My passport isn't here. I must have left it back at Ebenezer. I have to go back!"

I stared at him in disbelief. "What about the roadblocks? All hell is breaking loose out there!"

"But I have to have my passport to leave," Freddy said. He pulled me into a fierce hug. "I'll be back! I promise."

Time passed with agonizing slowness. I sat in the open courtyard of the guest house and watched the Haitian soldiers manning the roadblock on the street outside, armed to the teeth. I could hear gunfire, sometimes distant and sometimes nearby, and the clatter of helicopters overhead. Praying like never before, I begged God to protect Freddy. "God, in Your mercy, please bring Freddy back safely!"

In the wee hours of the following morning, God answered my prayer. Freddy appeared, passport in hand. At dawn, a ride was arranged to take us to the airport. And we experienced God's provision once again—there were no roadblocks on the way. We miraculously made our way safely to the Port-au-Prince airport.

Unexplainable mysteries and miracles continued. We were somehow motioned through lines with our outdated visas and airline tickets that may or may not have been canceled. We had no knowledge of what airline awaited us or if our tickets matched. We kept walking by faith, and I believe that, once again, angels ushered us onto a plane with destination U.S.A. God made a way home for us. That's the only explanation.

Upon reflection after returning to the United States, I wrote this in my Haiti journal: "God's call was not about helping women or building homes. It was about opening our eyes… moving our hearts. It was about renovating our souls. It was about letting go of things we thought necessary for happiness. It was about experiencing God when all else was taken away. He became our peace, provision, and protection—when all we had was *him*."

We had done none of the things we thought we were called to do, and yet I believe that all we went through was intended by God to prepare us for the next leg of our journey with Him. Our time in Haiti was not spent in vain.

Grace

We arrived home on Thanksgiving Day, 1987. My mother's small condo became our next home.

The following day, Freddy and I found ourselves in the Harris Teeter at a nearby shopping center. As I pushed the grocery cart down the fully stocked rows overflowing with fresh fruits and vegetables and a seemingly limitless variety of packaged foods, I began to shake uncontrollably. "So much. Oh my, we have so, so much," I whispered.

"Another time," said Freddy softly. "We'll come back later. Another day." We returned the empty cart and left the store.

Like a double-exposure, I pictured in my mind the abundance at Harris Teeter transposed against an image of the Haitian neighbors we had just left, particularly Elda and her children. I could see them as they prepared their sometimes only meal for the day—simple rice and beans with creole sauce on a dented tin plate.

May gratitude always fill our souls. May we always remember.

* * *

"Will there be a place for us to gather as a family for Christmas?" I asked God.

We had returned with the clothes in our few suitcases. We had no home and little money for gifts or decorations. "I want so much to be together again as a family. You know my desire. Please help!"

A few days later, as we continued to settle into Mother's two-bedroom condo, our friend Bob Wynne called.

"Guess what!" Bob said, barely able to contain his enthusiasm. "Do I have some good news for you! My friends Alan and Cathy Creedy just called and said they are leaving for the holidays to visit family. He asked me if your family might like to use their home in North Raleigh for the holidays. He says the house comes with a Christmas tree, poinsettias, and a refrigerator full of turkey and all the other food your family will need. He invited you to just enjoy it all for the week they are gone!"

Another amazing gift. I remember that Christmas morning in the Creedys' home as our family exchanged gifts. I must admit to feeling embarrassed at first, as Freddy and I had only a $10 gift budget for each person. But God caused me to remember Haiti once again, and my perspective transformed into one of gratitude. I was thankful that we *had* the $10 budget and reminded myself that it was *abundant*—much more than our friends in Haiti had. I was struck with the reality that abundance was not even what was important. Simply being together at last and sharing the love we had missed for the last five months was more than sufficient.

* * *

After the holidays, another gift came our way. Mildred and C.A. Dillon once again offered us their basement apartment to live in as we began to pray and seek God's guidance and direction for the next chapter of our journey.

Where Now?

"Where now, Lord? Are we there yet?"

We had returned from Haiti with no clear path ahead of us. We began to ask God some new questions. "Is there a place here in the United States where we might serve You? We want to follow You; will You lead us again? You answered our earlier prayers in order to change our hearts. We know we cannot go back to life as it was before Haiti. So—what now? Where now?"

We received some information about Urbana, the massive triennial student missions conference hosted by InterVarsity Christian Fellowship, which was scheduled to be held in Illinois over the last few days of 1987. Perhaps we'd find our answer there. So, along with 19,000 college students, Freddy and I registered for the event.

As we attended seminars and took in the inspiring words of the speakers—we even had the opportunity to dine at a round table with Tony Campolo—our underlying prayer was "Lord, show us a new path. Show us where You want us to serve You in the United States."

As we browsed among the vendor tables between seminar sessions, we discovered some potential construction options for Freddy. One that stood out was Habitat for Humanity. And so, soon after we returned to the basement apartment in Raleigh, we were packing our suitcases again, this time headed for an appointment we had arranged with Habitat at their headquarters in Americus, Georgia.

The day we were scheduled to leave for Georgia, the apartment telephone rang. It was a friend from the Urbana Conference.

"I know of your plans to travel to Georgia, and the thought came to me that a visit with Bob Lupton of Focused Community Strategies (FCS), an urban ministry in Atlanta, might be helpful. I've called Bob, and he's available to meet with you tomorrow afternoon if you're interested."

The next day, our 30-minute visit and interview with Bob Lupton resulted in an invitation to become interns with FCS in Atlanta for a year.

"As a builder, Freddy, you would serve in our Charis Community Housing Program," Bob said. "The program builds affordable homes for families who work alongside us—we call that 'sweat equity.' By putting their own efforts into the properties, they come away with a real sense of pride. It's not just charity. And, Helen, you would serve with Linda Langstratt in our Adopt-a-Grandparent Program. You'll be living in an inner-city Atlanta neighborhood, so you'll be learning to live in community with low-income families. I think you'll discover a real richness there. How does April sound?"

"That would work for us," Freddy replied. "Thank you, Bob, for this opportunity!"

As we were leaving, Bob said, "Welcome to the city! I will find you a rental and let the staff know of your upcoming service with us!"

Later I would read these words in Bob's book, *Theirs Is the Kingdom: Celebrating the Gospel in Urban America*: "The city, I have concluded, is a dangerous place to walk, especially for those of us who carry valuable baggage. Much of what we hold dear is likely to be stripped away. But for every loss there is a gain; something of greater value is given. That is part of the wealth of the inner city, and that is why Peggy and I have made the city our home."

We left Atlanta without seeing where we would live, without taking a tour of the community in which we would be serving. But God gave us a certainty and a peace that this was to be the next leg of our journey. We could trust God and Bob Lupton with the details.

New Holy Ground

After returning to Raleigh, we began organizing our lives for the move to Atlanta. We spent time with our financial and prayer partners with an eye to raising the funds necessary for our new mission budget. At one of the gatherings in the Dillon basement, our pastor, David Horner, said, "What would you think of, after interning with Bob Lupton in Atlanta, coming back here and setting up a similar inner-city ministry right here in Raleigh? We could set it up as a nondenominational nonprofit organization sponsored by local churches and individuals."

We were all silent for a moment, captivated by the idea. It felt like a God thing.

Finally, Freddy responded. "Let's all commit to pray about that suggestion during these next ten to twelve months and see what God reveals!"

So, with a plan for Atlanta and support raised, Freddy and I pulled out of the Dillon driveway for the last time on a spring day in 1988, ready for this new leg of the journey.

In the quiet of the U-Haul, I silently prayed, "Thank You, Lord, for opening the way for us to follow You in the U.S.A.!" Soft Christian music played on the radio over the hum of the road. For the third time in my life—as I was present to the Presence with me—I sensed these words: "Do you know how much I love you—how much I love you and Freddy?"

"Yes, Lord. You've proven that love for us over and over."

"Then come. Follow Me to Atlanta. Come feed My sheep. Feed My lambs, those who live on the margins, on this My holy ground. Come!"

Feed My Sheep

As we were approaching Atlanta, Freddy and I made a quick stop at a local grocery store to pick up a few essentials for our refrigerator and even some special ingredients for our "sweet tooth."

As the U-Haul pulled up to the small one-story house on Ormond Street in the Summerhill/Grant Park neighborhood just south of downtown Atlanta, my eyes were immediately drawn to the iron burglar bars shielding the front door and windows of what was to be our home for the next ten months.

We unloaded the U-Haul and began to unpack. As I emptied the boxes labeled KITCHEN, I discovered my beloved Bundt pan, a hand mixer, and all the measuring tools I used for baking. Cooking in the basement apartment in Raleigh and in the shared kitchen in Haiti had been limited to whatever I could do with a hot plate. I hadn't had an oven in either place. It was time, past time, to bake one of Freddy's favorites—a triple chocolate cake. I got started right away.

"Why don't we take a walk around the block while the cake cools," Freddy suggested. "Let's check out our new neighborhood!"

As we began our stroll down the street, we immediately noticed that most of the simple houses showed signs of needing some TLC. All had burglar bars just like ours.

As Freddy and I rounded the corner toward home, we noticed a young boy crossing the street. He was maybe eight or nine years old. Freddy, being Freddy, walked right up to the boy and said, "Hello! What's your name? My name is Freddy, and this is Helen."

"My name is Duke," he said with a broad smile.

"Nice to meet you, Duke," Freddy said. "We just moved in on this street. Our home is the one with lots of cardboard boxes on the front porch. Please come by to visit us any time."

We finished up our walk and went inside. No sooner had we shut the front door behind us than we heard a faint knock. Freddy opened the door and saw our new friend standing on the porch.

"Welcome, Duke. Come on in!"

Following me into the kitchen, the young boy caught sight of the chocolate cake resting on the kitchen counter.

"Is that a chocolate cake?" Duke asked.

"Yes," I answered. "Freddy just loves my chocolate cake, so I made one for him."

Still eyeing the cake, Duke said, "I bet I could eat a piece of that!"

"Well, I would be happy to cut you a piece," I responded. I cut a slice of the warm chocolate cake and passed it over to him. In just a few gulps, the piece of cake was all gone.

"Mm-mm, that was so good!" he said, and then added with a chuckle, "I bet I could eat another piece of that!"

"I'm so happy you enjoyed it," I said. "Here, let me get you another piece."

Finishing the second piece, Duke looked up with a bright smile of satisfaction. He leaned slightly toward me and said with a soft whisper, "Ms. Helen, I want to say thank you—because today is my birthday!"

My soul rejoiced. I heard the Spirit whisper to my heart: "Have no fear about what you are to do here in your new home in Atlanta. My request to feed My sheep, feed My lambs, will become clear. Be assured that I will send those to whom you are to give My love—with chocolate birthday cake and in other ways too!"

Love in Community

"What sheep, Lord? What lambs? Whom do we feed? How do we feed them?"

In simple, small ways, God began to reveal the who and the what and the how. Meeting neighbors was Freddy's first priority. He suggested that we make use of my home economics skills.

"How about baking a blueberry pie for the neighbors next door?"

"Perfect idea!" I agreed. I got to work immediately.

An hour or so later, I stood holding a still-warm pie on the narrow front porch of our neighbors' house. The paint on the front door was peeling. I knocked gently. A small girl opened the door and greeted me with a smile that showed a few missing front teeth.

"Hi," she said.

"Hello," I said. "My name is Helen. My husband, Freddy, and I just moved in next door. We hope you and your family like blueberry pie! And this note card has our telephone number on it, in case you need us for anything!"

She carefully took the pie and note card and placed them on a table just inside the door. She smiled again and politely said, "Thank you, Miss Helen. My name is Tammy."

* * *

Very little time passed before our neighbors took us up on our offer. Requests for small favors became frequent.

"Helen? This is Tammy's mom, Mrs. Wilson! I've just discovered that buying whole chickens at the grocery is cheaper than buying cut up ones. Would you show me how to cut up a chicken?" Or, "I have another request, Helen! Would you be willing to cut Tammy's hair? Every little bit of money we can save helps with our budget."

As we spent more time together, sharing our hopes and desires, we learned of the Wilson family's dreams of owning their own home someday.

As Freddy was working with FCS's Charis Community Housing Program, it was a natural thing for us to sponsor the Wilsons for a new, affordable home. The application was filled out and accepted. What a joy it was to join them in building up "sweat equity," helping them work toward their dream of home ownership. And when the small frame house was completed, what a privilege it was to celebrate together as they took possession of their very own home.

The Gospel of Neighboring

Our internship with FCS involved us in a variety of programs and experiences. While the majority of his time was spent building affordable houses with the Charis Community Housing Program, Freddy was also on call for emergencies within the FCS community. It was not unusual for him to receive calls for help at all hours.

"Freddy, can you get to Mrs. Bazemore's house right away? She's been burglarized. Her front door's been knocked out, and she needs it replaced right away—for her safety!"

My assignment was to serve with Linda Langstratt, director of the Adopt-a-Grandparent Program. This was the highlight of my week. Every Tuesday afternoon, we'd gather in one of the seniors' homes to share concerns, make plans, laugh, pray, and fellowship over hot tea and sugar cookies.

Behind our house was a low-income apartment building, and it provided a convenient target for our outreach. We developed relationships with the single moms and their young sons, eventually inviting them to participate: "Would you be willing for Travis to spend the night after pizza?" or "Would you permit Sam to go to Six Flags with us for the day?"

To provide a place for the energetic boys to play, Freddy set up a badminton net in our backyard. Soon our other neighbor, Mrs. Louise—a lonely 80-year-old widow—began to join in the fun and laughter. Whenever a badminton birdie would fly over the fence between our two yards, she'd slowly get out of her lawn chair, walk over, pick it up, and throw it back, chuckling each time.

We kept finding simple ways to feed God's sheep and lambs, offering love in fun and laughter, simply by being present. These small acts were all valued, as real community was being built.

A Lesson from Bessie

She entered the classroom, her arms cradling a bright orange plastic Jack-O-Lantern filled with five bags of Halloween candy and a large sheet of smiley-face stickers.

"Miss Bessie! Miss Bessie is here!" the children called out, some rushing to her side for a warm hug.

It was my treat to escort Miss Bessie, a beautiful 72-year-old friend from our neighborhood, to this elementary school in Decatur, Georgia. She was a participant in our FCS Adopt-a-Grandparent Program, and she served as a "grandmother" for Mrs. Miller's first grade class.

"I had always dreamed of becoming a teacher," Miss Bessie had shared with me on the way. "But my father worked on a farm, barely able to feed and care for his ten children. I guess there wasn't enough money for school and books."

As she read to the class, I could see that the children delighted in her. They loved her! In a very real way, Miss Bessie's dreams had finally come true.

Miss Bessie taught me to never give up on my dreams. But she also showed me the meaning of sacrifice. After she had finished her grandmother duties, Miss Bessie and I took a side trip to one of my favorite places in Atlanta—the Dekalb Farmers Market. As we walked the aisles, I began to fill my cart with homemade breads, delicious-looking cheeses, and assorted fruits.

"Can I help you find something, Miss Bessie?" I asked, after noticing her checking the price of fresh catfish and patting a ripe honeydew melon.

With a twinkle in her eye and a soft smile on her lips, she answered, "Well, Miss Helen, it's the end of the month. Money is kind of short. Guess I better not today."

It was then that I realized this sweet lady had just given all she had left that month so the children in her adopted class could have some Halloween candy!

Lord,

Thank You for Miss Bessie.

Thank You for You in Miss Bessie!

For in her sacrificial giving to the children and in denying herself,

You remind me, Lord, of Your sacrificial gift for me.

Teach me to be like Bessie, to be like You.

Teach me to give,

To give especially before my own wants and even needs are met.

Teach me to give not just out of my abundance,

Not just when I'm satisfied but,

When I want catfish and honeydew melon!

Help me to be like Bessie.

To be like You.

Do This for Me

Sunday morning at Georgia Avenue Church—such a wondrous mystery. Kneeling in the service of Holy Communion, taking broken bread and the cup of wine, remembering Christ's words: "Take, eat; this is My body which is given for you. Do this for the remembrance of Me."

I don't know that I fully understand the mystery of these elements, but I am aware that in obedience to *take* and *eat*, I am in communion with Christ. My heart is touched as the faces of the struggling people who are so much a part of our lives in Atlanta flash before my mind. The broken bodies of Christ.

"Take, these are given for you. Do this for Me!"

Thanks for the Service

On a cold, dreary February day, I drove toward Café 458, a nonprofit restaurant where I volunteered. The café invites people experiencing homelessness to come and be served a warm, free meal on tables laid with white cloths, real silverware, and vases of fresh flowers.

Along the way, I caught glimpses of poorly clad bodies huddled together in doorways, hoping for some protection from the wintry day. My heart ached, and my spirit felt a rush of guilt. I was in my warm car, clothed in a warm coat, coming from a warm house. Questions flooded my mind: "What good will chopping a few onions do? What difference will serving a few homeless people make? What am I here for?"

Still questioning my role, I pushed open the door of Café 458. The lights were off. Volunteers and staff stood in a circle praying quietly in the dark. Joining in, I prayed fervently for this unjust situation that plagues our land—homelessness. I prayed for the cold souls who would come in for a meal that day. I ask again: "Why am I here, Lord?"

At 11 a.m. the doors were opened. As our guests—those that our society tends to reject—entered, they were met with smiles, friendly greetings, and hot, delicious food.

I watched in awe as somehow, in just a brief space of time, in some mysterious way, a transformation took place in that sanctuary of warmth and hospitality. Seated at cloth-covered tables and served with love, the guests beamed radiant smiles.

"Why am I here?" I believe my question was answered when one of the elderly guests, as he picked up his hat to leave, turned my way and said, "Thanks, Miss. Thanks for the service."

He had come hungry, cold, and down—feeling unwanted. He left satisfied, warm, his spirit replenished—feeling cared for, respected, and loved. Transformation for a few moments!

Lord,

Thank You for that gentleman's words,

"Thanks for the service," which served as a reminder.

That I'm here as a servant serving You.

That coming to be with the poor brings me to You!

That being with Your children experiencing poverty

Allows me to see my own poverty.

Forgive my census-taking as I count the numbers needing to find love,

To be fed, clothed, housed, and valued.

Help me to see hope in that one You've given me this day,

Please bring help—one, two, fifty, and more—to be Your hands and feet and heart

To help break the chains of poverty, racism, injustice, and oppression.

Amen.

Holy Ground

During our time in Atlanta, Freddy and I made several trips back to Raleigh to meet with our support team. After much prayerful consideration and discernment, it was decided that we would indeed bring what we had been learning under Bob Lupton back to the Triangle, just as David Horner had suggested before we left. Though we didn't know exactly what it would look like, we began planning toward a non-denominational ministry among the underprivileged in downtown Raleigh.

On one of our last trips back—a weekend in April of 1989—Freddy and I planned to look for a new home in Raleigh. We prayed as we entered Wake County: "God, direct us to the place where we may follow Your call to 'feed Your sheep, feed Your lambs.'"

At a gas station on the outskirts of Raleigh, we bought a copy of The News & Observer, Raleigh's local newspaper. On the front page was an article about some old, condemned homes being torn down near the edge of the city center. The houses were no longer safe to live in, nor were they practical to restore. The demolition would leave eleven acres of vacant land adjacent to the old Pilot Mill and Halifax Court, a large public housing project.

At the time, Halifax Court was overridden with crime and poverty. Particularly notorious was "The Corner," the entrance into the complex off of North Blount Street. It was an area to be avoided. Most residents of Halifax were single moms on welfare trying to provide for their families under extremely trying circumstances. But we would come to learn that it was also a place of hope. As one of the resident mothers, Rita Wilkins, later told us: "Halifax Court is a strong community in the midst of crime and poverty. We have people who care and stick together to try to help our children the best we can."

"Perhaps we begin here," Freddy suggested, pointing at the article. He was already envisioning using his Civil Engineering degree and construction experience to build affordable housing on the newly vacant land.

We drove up and down the streets in and around Halifax Court searching for possible rental property. Freddy said, "Well, we wouldn't qualify for any of this government housing, but maybe there's an apartment nearby."

Then, just a block from the edge of Halifax Court, we spied a FOR SALE sign in the small front yard of a simple, one-story dwelling.

"Let's check it out," I suggested.

"Hon, the sign says FOR SALE not FOR RENT. We don't have the money for a down payment!"

"Let's take a look anyway!" I insisted.

As we walked up the rickety front steps onto the small front porch that had several wooden planks missing, I sensed God's spirit come over me. I understood immediately. *This is it!*

I held that revelation in my heart when we met soon after with our support team—friends who had given us the financial means and the prayerful backing we had needed to answer God's call in our lives. During our time together, Freddy and I shared the N&O article, our tour of the site, and the search for a home.

In all honesty I was overcome with emotion and teary eyes as I shared, "The hardest part of following Jesus for me has been leaving our family and giving up a home where our family could gather. Today, as we searched for a home, a rental, we did find a small house on East Franklin Street, not far from the vacant land mentioned in the article. It's also just a few blocks from Halifax Court, but it's not a rental. It's for sale. I'm not sure how we'd pay for it."

"How about we go with you to check it out?" Robert Boone said. "I'll contact the realtor, and we'll meet you there at 2:00 tomorrow."

In the quiet of the next morning as I sat with God, this scripture was in my daily devotion for this day: "But God led His own people forth like sheep and guided them with a shepherd's care like a flock in the wilderness. And He led them on safely and in confident trust, so that they feared not… and He brought them to His holy border" (Psalm 78:52–54).

As I held in my heart what God's word meant, that He would bring us to His holy border, I believed that He was going to give us a home near His children living on the margins. The house on E. Franklin was on the border! Just as being present with and living in community with the marginalized children of God in Haiti and inner-city Atlanta had been holy ground for Freddy and me, so too was this to be our new holy ground. I knew in my spirit even before we met with the realtor and our friends that somehow God was going to provide our new home on the border of our new holy ground.

Yes, God provides! Through these generous friends—Bob, Robert, Bill, and Tommy—a down payment was made. The FOR SALE sign became a SOLD sign!

Our new home, 204 East Franklin Street, was a historic house built in 1902. It was located within walking distance of the Governor's Mansion, the campus of Peace College, and Halifax Court. Across the street was a small, ill-kept shopping strip. We knew the house would take a lot of work, but we were so grateful for a place where we could once again welcome our family and friends. And we looked forward to the prospect of pouring into the lives of our new neighbors and learning from them.

The Gift of Home

When we moved into the little house on Franklin Street, we discovered 24 cracked or missing windowpanes. I laughingly said to Freddy, "You know, this is really no big problem. We learned in Haiti that we could survive without windows *or* doors. And there we survived with mosquitoes, rats, and scorpions. This place is pure luxury! And far nicer than the way most of God's children live."

The kitchen had a small upright stove with a missing oven door handle. But again, we couldn't complain. After all, we had managed with just a hot plate in our basement apartment and in our room in Haiti. Four burners and an oven? Wow, what a blessing!

The ceiling was low and stained, only two cabinet drawers actually worked, and the enamel kitchen sink was streaked with rust. But we had running water, so no complaints from us! Little by little we began to build our nest, our own home, as our children returned our furniture and other household goods. Some of our things had been destroyed in a fire at an old farmhouse our son Kent had been renting while he was attending East Carolina University. Friends pitched in to fill in the gaps.

The house had no air conditioning, so we kept the windows open for some slight relief from the early heat of May. The open windows also let in the sound of gunfire from Halifax Court, especially in the evenings. I was reminded of the gunfire I had heard during the nights in Haiti. God had protected us in Haiti. We knew God would protect us in inner-city Raleigh as well.

God's Plan Revealed

As we lay in our bed that first morning in our new home, I turned toward Freddy.

"Good morning! How was your night?"

"Perfect!" said Freddy, with his usual "glass completely full" attitude. "How did you sleep?"

"I had a very restful night," I replied. "I certainly don't miss the constant blaring sirens of Atlanta. It seems pretty quiet here."

I pushed myself up on one elbow and continued. "I do remember having a very vivid dream. I heard voices talking about names. They were asking about a possible name for God's ministry here. How does Building Together Ministries sound to you?"

"I like it. I really like it!" he said, leaning over to plant a kiss on my cheek. "That's it! We have a place and a name—a real beginning!"

He jumped out of bed and started getting dressed. "While you get back to unpacking, I'm going to stroll around the block, maybe meet some neighbors. While I'm out, I'll pick up some hot doughnuts from the Krispy Kreme around the corner. We'll have our first breakfast at 204!"

We were excited, but we were still clueless. I remember praying during my quiet time later that same day: "What now, Lord? Do we print T-shirts that say BTM? Do we knock on doors and announce, 'Hi! We're the Johnsons, your new neighbors! How may we serve you?' Lord, we don't know what we're doing! Please help!"

As He always had before, God opened the way through natural and simple steps. We took time to visit the shops across the street. We met a few neighbors and some of the residents of Halifax Court. We made an appointment at the office of the Raleigh Housing Authority, just a block away. While there, Freddy said to Steve Beam, the director: "We are the Johnsons, new residents in the neighborhood. We intentionally moved here in order to serve with folks in this community. We plan to establish a nonprofit organization called Building Together Ministries, complete with a board of directors and 501(c)(3) status. Our home will be our office for now. We are available. Please call on us for any needs we might help with."

"Well, welcome to the neighborhood, Johnsons!" Mr. Beam replied. "We will be calling on you, I'm sure. So good to get help!"

Walking along the nearby streets became a habit. To any neighbors we saw sitting on their front stoops we offered introductions, handshakes, and an invitation: "Our home is at 204 E. Franklin Street. Our doors will be open every Sunday evening at 7:00 p.m. for singing, prayer, and just getting to know one another. You and your friends and family are most welcome." We extended the same invitation for the Sunday night gatherings to friends across town from all walks of life. All were welcomed. And many came, some from Raleigh's wealthier neighborhoods, and some from the local community, some walking and some driving. On Sunday evenings, our small living room was filled with song and praise, laughter and tears.

We learned later that our new next-door neighbor, John Baily, an interior designer, had tried to describe the gatherings to mutual friends. "I see Mercedes and beat up pickup trucks both parked at 204 E. Franklin on Sunday evenings. I'm not really sure what's going on over there!"

When the weather was nice, we sometimes took prayer walks with various folks, including some from the Sunday night group. We would stroll down Blount Street, along the edge of the housing project, stopping to pray here and there. One evening, a patrol car pulled up beside us. The officer rolled down the window and said, "I'd suggest you take your afternoon exercise elsewhere. This is a very dangerous neighborhood!"

Heart Surgery

Just as Freddy and I needed to clean up the space in our new home on Franklin Street to make it hospitable for family and the community we had joined, God knew we needed to clean up some dark spaces in our hearts also. A key part of this internal house-cleaning journey had to do with my attitudes about race.

As we began our life in the inner city of Raleigh, our Atlanta friend Bob Lupton would check in on us every few weeks to see how our transition was going. During one of our conversations, Bob said, "I have a suggestion for you. Dr. John Perkins of Voice of Calvary Ministries in Jackson, Mississippi, is offering a conference for folks called to relocate to inner-city neighborhoods, just like the two of you."

He went on to tell us a bit about John and his wife, Vera Mae, and the amazing story of how God had called this African American couple in 1960 to move from Pasadena, California, back to the poor rural area of Mendenhall, Mississippi, to start a ministry among the people there, and how this had led eventually to the establishment of Voice of Calvary.

"This conference might be another great learning opportunity for you both," he concluded. "I'll send you the registration information."

We thanked Bob for the suggestion and soon decided to attend. When the time came, we eagerly drove the distance to Mississippi. We were expecting to receive lists of useful resources, tips from experienced inner-city workers, and lots of ideas to better equip us for urban ministry. Little did we know that God had a very different agenda in mind for clueless Helen and Freddy.

I clearly remember the love and the warm welcome we received from John and Vera Mae. We felt immediately at ease. As the conference began, the Perkinses shared the story of being called back to their roots in Mississippi. At first, their ministry had simply consisted of sharing the gospel with 1,500 public school children every month. Then God brought helpers, and they started a daycare center, a youth program, a church, a thrift store, a health center, and even an adult education program. Our souls were filled with wonder and awe and dreams as we listened. "Maybe that's what Building Together might become!"

The weekend also featured stories from others connected to Voice of Calvary, including Chris Rice and Spencer Perkins, John's son. Spencer and Chris had met when Chris came to serve as a volunteer at VOC. When the time had come to return to college, Chris found himself struggling with a question: "What do I want to make of my Christian life?" Chris chose to stay and become a part of the community. The two men, one black and one white, together with their families, ended up living in a large community house called Antioch. They lived, worked, worshiped, and dealt with race "face on."

Our group was challenged in so many ways by the stories we heard. John, Vera Mae, Spencer, and Chris invited us to personally engage in critical self-reflection and evaluation about our own understanding of the meaning of race and our whiteness.

Years later, Spencer and Chris would write the following: "Our need to admit that we wear racial blinders is similar to an alcoholic's need to admit that he has the disease of alcoholism. Alcoholics have a natural tendency to abuse alcohol. Initially confronted, an alcoholic will swear up and down that he doesn't drink too much and that he can control himself. The first and most critical step on the road to recovery is for the alcoholic to admit that he has a problem (some say admitting is 70% of the solution) and that he can't manage his problem without God's help. He knows that if he lets down his guard and forgets what his inherent weakness is, he'll slide into abuse again. The introduction that Alcoholics Anonymous members use in their meetings, 'My name is Joe, and I'm an alcoholic,' recognizes that inherent tendency to abuse alcohol. We whites need to come to the point where we can say, 'My name is Chris, and I've been wearing racial blinders.' Admitting this helps me remember that, left to my own devices, I will look out for me and mine first. Only by admitting our blinders can we begin the process of stripping them away, piece by piece."[9]

I began to realize that I had lived much of my life in a bubble. I had lived in a space of ignorance. I had lived with blinders that kept me from seeing the racial issues that existed all around me. For the first time, I wrestled with the phrase "white privilege." In her groundbreaking 1989 essay "White

Privilege: Unpacking the Invisible Knapsack," the activist Peggy McIntosh described white privilege as "an invisible package of unearned assets which I can count on cashing in every day, but about which I was meant to remain oblivious." At that moment, I began to see the white privilege that I had been oblivious to throughout my entire life.

I thought back to my childhood, where the "N" word was part of my father's daily conversations. I had been taught that I was superior to people of color. People of color were "over there" and were to be avoided. It was *us* and *them*. And I could see many examples through the years of my path being made easier because of my whiteness.

But as Freddy and I sat listening in this community of black and white leaders in Mississippi, my initial reaction still was one of defensiveness. "I can certainly see and acknowledge my white privilege," I thought, "but surely I'm not considered a racist! Not me! Why, look at us, Freddy and me! We were the minority living in the black culture of Haiti. And give us stars on our forehead—we just spent a year in a mixed, inner-city community in Atlanta. And, really, we don't don white hoods or burn crosses in yards, and we certainly don't say the 'N' word! Racist? Nope. Not us!"

As we continued to reflect, however, we felt a clear prompting in our souls from the spirit of God. We began to ask ourselves some tough questions. Where were we, where were our hearts, as we watched on TV the brutality of police toward black humanity, when they suffered under fists, clubs, dogs, fire hoses, bombs? Where were we? We sat there thinking that it wasn't our problem. It was happening somewhere else. Where were our hearts when we first learned of Raleigh school integration? What was our first gut reaction to this news? Freddy and I both said, "We must enroll our children in private school!" And why did we treat our domestic help—her name was Rachael—with such lack of involvement, such distance? We had hired her when our kids were little, and I would begin each week by passing on the long list of cleaning needs. Did I ever think to ask the names of her children or the date of her birthday? Did I ever invite her to join me at the kitchen table for a morning cup of coffee? And where did my fear come from that I didn't attend her funeral? Perhaps it was the realization that I had never had a real relationship outside of my white comfort zone. We began to understand that we had better check our spirit of superiority as we began life in the inner city. We certainly were not the white saviors we thought we were, coming to save a poor black community!

These questions revealed that our true hearts needed major surgery. From the Perkinses and Chris Rice we learned the mantra "ADMIT, SUBMIT, COMMIT."[10] For the duration of the retreat, new awareness led to confessions, which led to tears. Tears brought us to deep conversations and prayers, pleading for forgiveness. Racial reconciliation continues to be an ongoing "admit, submit, commit" process in my soul.

The Jackson conference was just the beginning of God's renovation of our souls. We had much to learn as we faced what God wanted to change within us. This was just the start. Before going on to help others, someone has remarked "should we not confess our blindness regarding the dynamics of white privilege in our own backyard?"

We left Mississippi with a new vision, a vision captured in a Chinese poem John Perkins read to us at the conclusion of the conference:

> *Go to the people*
> *Live among them*
> *Learn from them*
> *Love them*
> *Start with what you know*
> *Build on what they have*
> *But of the best leaders,*
> *When the task is done,*
> *The people will remark*
> *"We have done it ourselves."*

With our souls having been made freshly and acutely aware of our own biases and racism, Freddy and I left the conference committed to sharing these truths with others in our home city of Raleigh. We had a genuine desire that our friends' eyes would be opened as ours had been. We wanted to be tools used by God to bring about racial healing.

But how does one begin to work toward racial reconciliation in an urban neighborhood in a Southern city? We began by inviting the very people who had inspired us, people such as Dr. John Perkins, Chris Rice, Spencer

Perkins, and others, to lead racial reconciliation conferences in Raleigh. We hoped that white folks would leave these events with the question, "What do we do now?"

On a smaller scale, Building Together Ministries began organizing mixed-race lunch and dinner groups. These groups would alternate between black and white members' homes to fellowship over a shared meal, usually accompanied by a book or Bible study. Many new cross-community relationships began to develop.

Sometimes it's as simple as bringing folks together. Father Gregory Boyle, a Jesuit priest and the founder of Homeboy Industries, the largest gang-intervention program in the world, says in his book *Tattoos on the Heart—The Power of Boundless Compassion*: "When we are together, we discover the reservoir of life whose richness is hard to see when we are apart and isolated."[11]

Chris Rice and Emmanuel Katongole, in their 2008 book *Reconciling All Things—A Christian Vision for Justice, Peace and Healing*, explain, "The journey of reconciliation is difficult, daily work. In the face of the long haul, inevitably the question comes: Why bother? 'For the joy set before Him,' the Scriptures tell us, 'Jesus endured the cross.' The long haul must eventually become marked by the pursuit of joy."[12]

On this leg of our journey of reconciliation, I found that Jesus was making himself known to me in new ways. We found a new richness in living life together with neighbors from whom we had been separated. That's joy worth pursuing!

The Voice of Community Needs

W e had returned to Raleigh from Mississippi with the encouragement and challenges we had received from John Perkins, Chris Rice, and others. "Go to the people, live among them, learn from them, love them, and *listen, listen, listen.*"

Our earlier visits to the local office of Raleigh Housing Authority brought results. We received an encouraging phone call.

"Mrs. Johnson, this is Peggy Dublin. I'm the president of the Resident's Association of Halifax Court. I would like to invite you and your husband to our Tuesday night meeting at the Halifax Rec Center."

We promised we would be there. We believed more and more strongly that God was directing our steps toward Halifax. And this meeting would give us a chance to listen.

We arrived at the rec center not really knowing what to expect. Peggy began the meeting by asking us to introduce ourselves to the fifteen or so single mothers gathered in the large conference area.

"Thank you for inviting us to your meeting," Freddy said. "We are Freddy and Helen Johnson, your new neighbors at 204 East Franklin Street. We're happy to meet you, and we're eager to listen to your stories and find out about your hopes and dreams for this community. We hope to become friends and to learn how we might work together for Halifax Court."

One of the moms, a young woman named Barbara Steadman, immediately raised her hand. "I can tell you a need of mine and I think of other moms here. My oldest child, my son Roderick, needs a mentor. How about starting a big brother/big sister program? Would you help us help our children?"

And there, clear as day, was God's initial plan for Building Together Ministries—not building affordable houses or creating businesses, but *helping the mothers help their children.*

With that we had a name, a clearer idea, and a first tangible request from the neighborhood. Our second bedroom became the BTM office, and we got down to the business of setting up an urban nonprofit. We planned to keep our supporters informed with a regular newsletter telling the God stories of the city.

At about this time, Stan Wiebe—our Canadian missionary friend from Haiti—contacted us as he was finishing up his Haiti commitment. "Freddy, I think God is calling me to work with youth in the inner city!"

"Well, come on. We could certainly use your help with the youth programs we're planning and also with our accounting books."

Stan moved into the neighborhood, just two doors down from our home. He became the director of "The Friends," BTM's big brother/big sister mentorship program. God was answering Barbara Steadman's prayer. Roderick, her son, would have a mentor soon!

Volunteer Help Provided

Our small front porch on E. Franklin became an "altar" of sorts, as friends from all parts of the city would leave used clothes and various home furnishings to help with the ministry. We needed a way to turn the donated items into cash. Peace College, located just one block away, granted us permission to use their baseball field for monthly yard sales. Neighbors from Halifax Court were eager to volunteer and help us with the sales, knowing that the proceeds would directly fund the program the community had requested—The Friends!

We were encouraged by the donations of furnishings, clothes, and money, of course, but most encouraging of all were the offers to serve. We knew that a question like "How can we help 'hands on'?" would likely lead to the building of relationships, to new friendships. One of the first such calls came from two Raleigh businessmen, Tommy Drake and Ruffin King.

"What's an immediate need in the community today?" they asked.

We called Steve Beam at the Raleigh Housing Authority. "What's your greatest need? We have two able-bodied men wanting to volunteer."

"Well, Johnny's apartment at 700 Blount Street could use some attention," the director replied.

Tommy later told the story of that first volunteer outing: "Not long after Freddy and Helen founded BTM, volunteers were given the opportunity to serve the residents of Halifax Court, a local housing complex. When the Saturday workday arrived, Ruffin King and I were assigned to an elderly resident named Johnny whose disabilities prevented him from adequately cleaning his apartment, his linens, or his clothes. There was no bathroom on his ground floor, only a small den and kitchen. He had difficulty walking, much less using stairs. Due to his infirmities, he would use what was called a 'slop bucket' to relieve himself during the day. He would only climb the stairs at bedtime when he would haul the bucket up the stairs to empty it in the toilet.

Johnny was a colorful character and seemed quite happy to have us spend time with him that day. His den furniture consisted of one old recliner chair, a side table with a bird cage on it, and a small TV. A pet parakeet rested on his shoulder the entire time we worked to clean his apartment. Johnny sat in his recliner eating his favorite ice cream as he talked to us and the parakeet.

After three or four hours of scrubbing and cleaning, Ruffin and I were ready for a lunch break, but when we opened his closet, we found a pile of dirty clothes on the floor (nothing was hanging in the closet.) We gathered up his sheets, towels, and clothes and headed for the laundromat on Franklin Street across from the Johnson home. We loaded and started three machines with ample Tide. I lifted the machine lids to check on the progress. 'Look, Ruffin. The water looks like chocolate milk!' It took two more wash cycles to get them clean.

I was convicted of how I took for granted having clean clothes and a clean home. My heart opened to the fact that those who live on the margins do not have the availability of resources or the ability to care for themselves adequately.

After running everything through the dryers, we folded his now clean belongings and returned to Johnny's home. He was still sitting in his recliner where we'd left him, watching TV with his bird on his shoulder. We bid farewell to our new friend with plans to return for a visit someday.

Ruffin and I reflected on the impact Johnny left in our hearts. Our brief visit gave witness to a soul who, despite his lack of family or material possessions, was a man who was joyful and light-hearted even in hard circumstances. I can honestly say that we intended to bless Johnny with our efforts. However, it is Johnny who blessed us simply by his presence."

Shared Gifts

L ife in our new/old house came with many renovating issues. An immediate problem that needed to be addressed was flooding and standing water in the dirt-floor basement. Among our neighbors on E. Franklin Street was a group of concrete finishers—Squeaky, James, and Leon—who had moved up from New Orleans to work at the Raleigh-Durham Airport. Squeaky was the one who became our neighborhood "watchdog." Whenever he was at home, he kept a careful eye on our house.

When the basement flooding started, Freddy immediately walked the three doors up the street and knocked on the door. "Hey, Squeaky. We have a real problem at our house. With all this rain, our basement is filled with water. Have you ever put in a sump pump?"

"I'm your man, Mr. Johnson," Squeaky said. "Let me know when, and I can help any day after work."

Within the week, Freddy and Squeaky were at work installing the pump. I listened as their voices floated up the stairs. I overheard conversations about growing up in Louisiana and North Carolina, and stories of jobs and family. After the pump was installed, they came up and sat at our kitchen table for lemonade and cookies.

"I can't thank you enough," Freddy said. "I never could have done this by myself. Such a great job! Let's settle up now. What do I owe you, Squeaky?"

"Naw, man, Mr. Freddy. Are you kidding? There's no charge. *Y'all are my neighbors!*"

An Uninvited Guest

Our nights on E. Franklin Street were often subject to noisy interruptions. Raised voices, passing sirens, and knocks on the front door were not uncommon. One weekend I was awakened by a different sound, one that I quickly realized was coming from inside the house rather than outside.

"Freddy!" I whispered as I shook him awake. "Someone is in our living room! I just heard the squeak of the antique cupboard. Someone opened the door of the hutch!"

"You're dreaming again," he said. "Go back to sleep!"

No sooner had the words come out of his mouth than we both heard the squeaking sound.

"Hear it? Someone is in there!"

Freddy sat straight up in bed in the darkness. "My phone is in the office. I can't call 911!"

After a few tense moments, he came to a decision. He took a deep breath and yelled: "If anyone is in our home, would you please go out the way you came in? Peacefully, please!"

No response came. The house was silent.

"Helen, I'm going to have to go into the office so I can call 911. Just pray!"

He made his way into the room directly across from our bedroom. I was so scared I went into the small bathroom off our bedroom, locked the door, and got on my knees to pray. Within a few minutes, the beams of flashlights outside gave indication that the police had arrived. Freddy answered their knock on the front door and with their protection entered the living room. The antique cabinet door was standing open. The TV inside was undisturbed. The beam of the policeman's flashlight landed on the sofa. Sprawled across it, our uninvited guest was sound asleep in his underwear.

"We've run into this gentleman in the bars downtown all night. I guess he'd had enough and needed a place to chill. Do you want to press charges?"

"Oh no," we both chimed in. "We guess he's just one of our neighbors. We'll be intentional about locking our doors from now on, so as not to tempt uninvited guests!"

You Are Here to Stay

"God, how do we begin to build trust? How can this community trust a white couple that just… showed up? Lord, would You send me one friend, one relationship? Might we begin with one relationship?"

Word quickly traveled into the community that this white couple was offering help and inviting folks to prayer and praise on Sunday nights in their home on E. Franklin Street. So, knocks on our front door soon followed. People asked for change, for bus fare, for milk, for diapers. Rides to doctors' offices were common requests. One morning when I responded to another knock, a lovely lady stood on the front doormat with her arm extended for a handshake.

"Good morning!" she said. "I am Teresa. I live just down the street. I am your neighbor!"

"Hello, neighbor. I'm Helen. Won't you come in?" I offered with a smile. She followed me into the living room, and we sat together on the sofa. Her eyes roamed the room, settling on some family photos propped on a nearby table.

"I see you have three children, Helen. I have two boys myself, and they would like to be in the Friends Program. I came to welcome you, but—honestly—I also came to check you out. You know, we have a lot of people come and go all the time around here. Well-intended church groups bring meals or ice cream in the summer for the kids, but then they are gone."

Her eyes looked down to the navy and white fabric of the sofa. She reached down and began to softly pat the cushion. She looked up with a smile and said, "But you—you are here to stay."

I felt something deep within me. "I hope, Teresa, that you will be my friend. I need you."

A Plaid Miracle

"God, is this Helen and Freddy's idea and vision, or is it *Your* plan and vision?"

This question became central to our prayers as we listened to our neighbor's voices in the early days of the ministry.

An early morning call came in from a friend in North Raleigh. "I just read your monthly newsletter and your list of donation needs. I have a very good sofa bed I would like to donate. Do you know of anyone that could use it? I would love for it to find a home in Halifax Court!"

I immediately thought of my neighbor Louise. I knew that her son was due to be coming out of incarceration in a few weeks. This might be the perfect provision for him.

"Why, yes, thank you!" I replied. "I know just the person."

I made the necessary arrangements. On the day the sofa was to be delivered, I strolled over to Louise's apartment. I arrived just in time to see the bulky item being wrestled through her front door by the volunteer movers. Louise was standing excitedly on her front stoop. When she saw me, she threw her hands up in the air and shouted, "Well! The Lord sure knows what He's doing!"

I was puzzled by her remark, but her excitement was contagious. I followed her across the threshold into the living room. What I saw froze me in awe. In the corner of the room was a large club chair upholstered in the identical brown-and-gold plaid material as the donated sofa bed!

"Yes, Louise," I thought to myself, rejoicing. "The Lord surely does know what He's doing… down to the very last detail… even matching plaids!"

In that moment, a tender voice echoed in my heart. "Helen, you can depend on Me. I'm always ready to reveal what's next for My work here. Just seek and wait and listen."

HELP Answered

As we continued to honor the practice of listening to our neighbors, it became clear that educational support was a primary need among the households of Halifax Court. To provide for this need, we envisioned an after-school tutoring program and a computer lab. And the list grew to include a thrift store, camps, and more. "Help, Lord" again became my daily prayer.

So far, all programs were taking place at 204 E. Franklin Street and at Stan's rental at 208 E. Franklin Street. "Lord, I think I can handle this wonderful chaos for maybe six more months. Please help! Building Together needs more space!"

Shortly after my prayer for space, we received a phone call from Judy Hoffman, a member of our church who was also a member of the Wake County Board of Education.

"Helen, would you and Freddy be open to a visit from some of the members of the Board of Education? I was sharing with them about your beginning work in the Halifax Court community. They are interested in hearing about your vision."

"Well, I'm not sure how much we have to tell in these early stages," I replied, "but we can certainly tell our story and talk about God's clear call. How does next Tuesday afternoon sound? Say 2:00?"

"Putting it on my calendar!" Judy said. "See you then."

The following Tuesday a small group including several members of the school board sat together in our small living room. Freddy and I shared our faith journey that had led us to downtown Raleigh and Halifax Court.

"When we relocated here, we were advised to spend time building relationships and just listening to our neighbors. It's easy for outsiders to see needs and to come up with 'solutions.' But we believe that the important move is to simply listen and learn your neighbors' thoughts, desires, and dreams. For example, it was at a meeting with moms from the community that we heard the phrase 'Help us help our children,' and that led to the establishment of our big brother/big sister Friends Program. We believe that spiritual, emotional, and educational support programs will be welcomed by the community too. At this time we don't know what those will look like, or where they will take place. But we believe God will provide."

Judy spoke up. "Well, we think you should request the vacated Barbee School at 1600 Blount Street. It's right across the street from Halifax Court and would offer just the space you need."

"That's a great idea," Freddy agreed, "but we honestly don't have anywhere near the funds to buy a whole school!"

"But you don't understand," Judy said. "This is a really amazing deal. The school board is leasing vacated schools for $1.00 a year! I think you could afford that! The only requirement would be to meet with the board to explain your plan for the use of the property."

With the encouragement of our guests, Freddy and I agreed to appear before the Wake County Board of Education to share our community's vision to help the mothers help their children. Building Together Ministries was granted the space we had prayed for—truly a gift! The old Barbee Elementary School and its four acres of land was ours for a grand total of $1.00 per year.

God is always ready, we were learning, to answer our prayers beyond what we could even imagine.

Hospitality House

"Let me run an idea by you that I had during my quiet time this morning," said our good friend Bob Wynne. "You know Maggie and I have been in a Bible study at Providence—Henry Blackaby's *Experiencing God.* This week's study was about listening for God's call on your life by looking to places where you see God working and then becoming involved in that place. Building Together is that place for us. And we just heard from a realtor at church that the house next door to you—John Bailey's home and business on the corner of Blount and Franklin—is coming on the market. So, we're praying about selling our house and joining you on Franklin Street!"

"Best idea I've heard in a long time!" exulted Freddy. "Come on down!"

Maggie and Bob's new home at 730 Blount Street became Building Together's Hospitality House. Through the generosity of the Wynnes, the house was used for fellowship gatherings, Bible studies, weddings, parties for celebrating birthdays, room and board for invited speakers like Dr. John Perkins, Bob Lupton, and others, covered dish gatherings for neighbors, and much more.

During one of the early events at the Wynne house, we found out that, despite our sincere commitment to racial healing, bumps in the road would still come along. It was a fall weekend, and we had invited our BTM Board of Directors to join a group of community neighbors for an evening of covered dishes of home-cooked Southern foods. We hoped for a fruitful time of fellowship and getting to know one another.

Maggie Wynne, the hostess, and I stood at the front door and greeted the arriving guests. One of our senior neighbors from Halifax Court, Mrs. Josie, stepped gingerly across the threshold holding a huge pot of her famous collard greens. I watched as Maggie said, "Oh, it's Mrs. Josie, the collard lady! May I help you with your pot?"

She took the pot and headed off toward the kitchen. As I stood watching, Mrs. Josie's brow furrowed, and her soft smile quickly turned into a hard line across her face. I quickly raced to catch up with Maggie.

"Oh my gosh, Maggie, I think you've offended Mrs. Josie. I think when you referred to her as 'the collard lady' she heard you say 'the colored lady' instead! Judging by her expression, I think she's pretty upset."

The two of us quickly approached Mrs. Josie. With honest explanations and heartfelt apologies given, laughter followed, and smiles were renewed. We were neighbors becoming reconciled.

Servants in Service

God had abundantly answered our prayers for space in which to do his work. He had provided an entire elementary school for the BTM programs and the Wynnes' lovely brick home for hospitality events. Then we prayed for direction concerning our place of worship and were led to join—and integrate—Halifax Missionary Baptist Church, which was located just a block away from the BTM NeighborCenter. Our next prayer: "God, would You send the workers we need for Your growing programs here? And would You send diverse, committed servants? We definitely don't want to be seen as a *white* ministry."

Delores Steele Richardson was a member of the church, and she taught Sunday School there for almost 12 years. She tells me she remembers the Sunday two new students arrived in her class. They were, quite obviously, white. She recalls that the pastor later introduced us to the congregation as "missionaries from Providence Baptist Church who will be attending here."

"That was how I was introduced to BTM," Delores said. "It was already a time of frustration for me, as I desired a church outreach into the Halifax neighborhood. I heard God say, 'These are people you can partner and serve with, and I did.'"

Freddy would later say that Delores was the best teacher he ever had. She would go on to serve on BTM's Board of Directors for five years, including one year as chairperson. She transitioned to the position of Executive Director of BTM in 1995.[13]

* * *

As we strolled through the neighborhood, we visited The Halifax Court Child Development and Family Services Center, inviting staff to join us for Sunday evening prayer gatherings at our home. Linda Hawkins was one of the invitees.

The following Sunday, Linda was part of the gathering. She confessed later, "I came to investigate this white couple who were walking around knocking on doors in a predominantly black neighborhood. They won my approval."

Linda[14] began to volunteer and then heard God's call to be on staff. She joined Stan[15] who was already part of our growing group.

The next new staff member arrived soon afterward. I'll always remember the day she swept into our halls. With her reddish, stylish hairdo and radiant, soft brown skin, she was a "sparkle." She held out her hand and said, "Hello, my name is Reggie Edwards!"[16]

Before I could even share my name, she wrapped me in a huge hug. "I've been looking for you for some time. I'm so glad to be here! I've been knocking on the doors of churches for the last couple of months, challenging pastors to move beyond their church building walls and go into the communities 'to be the church for those in need.' Finally, a pastor, tired of me knocking on his door, said, 'I think I know of a place like you are talking about. It's in an old school building in downtown Raleigh. Let me take you there.' And so he did. And here I am!"

I took her hand as we walked down the hall toward the corner room on the first floor, chattering all the way. The room was furnished with donated sofas and upholstered club chairs. It was a space where women could meet, share, shed tears, laugh, and pray. We called it "My Sister's Place."

From those first meetings onward, Linda, Reggie, Delores, and I have been sisters. And Stan was like a son to us. God was sending His servants, and He continued to do so through the years with key contributors like Anna Neal Blanchard, Erin Kesterson Bowers, Sharon and Jim Bright, Vicky Chapman, Marcella Hamilton, Warren Keyes, Andrea Shrum Long and Skip Long, Matthew Long, Liz Rice, Kelly McInnes Swanson, Nancy Swope, and Wanda Worrell, among many others.

The Presence of Love

The used blue van was a gift from supporters who heard of our needs as programs and adventures were developed for the youth of the community. Over the years, the blue van traveled to youth conferences in New York, to Kids Across America in Branson, Missouri, to Urban Young Life Camp in Florida, to Windy Gap and Camp Sea Gull in North Carolina, and to many other places in between.

After returning from an Urban Youth Retreat at Windy Gap, Freddy shared a conversation he'd had with one of the African American leaders as they enjoyed the warmth of a hot tub under the cold, starry night sky of the North Carolina mountains.

"I shared with Charles that, as a white man, I really felt out of place among all the young black campers. I told him that I didn't know why I was there," Freddy said. "But my new acquaintance replied, 'Freddy, these black youth need to see and know a white man who loves them. Your presence is so important!'"

A Lesson from a Volunteer

One morning as I opened our front door to welcome God's life lessons for the day, a station wagon pulled up to the curb in front of our house. I immediately recognized the radiant, sparkling smile of my friend Anne. I could also see that the back of her car was loaded with toys. My heart was encouraged as I thought of all the fun the children of Halifax Court would have with these gifts.

As she placed the boxes loaded with toys, children's books, and a doll house on our front porch, Anne said, "Helen, I'm sorry that I haven't been able to volunteer more. It's just not God's timing for me to be involved hands-on with Building Together."

She proudly pointed to her two precious preschoolers seated in their car seats.

"However, I might be able to help in other ways. What are some other things besides children's toys you need for the community? I would be happy to pass on a list to my friends and church in North Raleigh!"

"Children's clothes!" I quickly responded. "Always children's clothes. And, oh yes, right now I have a particular need for a size 14 wedding dress and a gold wedding band."

I was thinking of the upcoming wedding of my neighbor and friend, Joann.

Anne's forehead wrinkled. "A gold ring?"

"Yes, a wedding ring!" I answered.

Anne paused. Then with one quick, decisive motion, she reached down with her right hand and slid from the fourth finger of her left hand her engagement ring, leaving a simple gold wedding band on her finger.

"Oh, no! I can't take this," I said as she gently placed the ring in the palm of my hand.

"Please. Take it!" she said. "I have two!"

"If you have two coats," he replied, "give one to the poor. If you have extra food, give it away to those who are hungry." (Luke 3:11; *The Living Bible*)

Ministry Highlight

Throughout the day, excitement filled the air as neighbors and friends joined in to prepare 730 N. Blount Street for the wedding of our neighbors Joann Ezell and Charles McNeill. The Wynnes' living room furniture had been carefully transported into storage in the BTM NeighborStore's truck to make room for fifty white rental chairs. Freshly ironed lace tablecloths draped the tables in the dining and breakfast rooms. Pink summer fruit punch and homemade delectables of ham biscuits, sandwiches, sausage balls, iced chocolate brownies, deviled eggs, cheese crisps, and more were gifts for the reception from the BTM Women's Bible Study. Two white feather doves perched on top of the beautifully decorated three-tier buttercream and vanilla wedding cake. Arrangements of flowers in jewel hues of deep purples, reds, and blues had been lovingly assembled and placed on the mantle, banister, and tables, and in the bouquets and boutonnieres of the wedding party. Vases with Queen Anne's lace offered additional soft touches of grace and beauty for this special occasion. A musician from nearby Halifax Baptist Church played melodiously as the guests began to arrive.

As the ceremony started, I thought in amazement, "What a miracle! God has truly done a work in this neighborhood!"

Everyone came—neighbors from the inner city and neighbors from the suburbs—dressed in their very best. One couldn't tell rich from poor. And the bridal party was especially handsome as a mixture of black and white bridesmaids and groomsmen stood beside the bride and groom.

"This is what heaven will be like!" I thought. "Yes. Young and old, rich and poor, black and white coming together with a common purpose— to praise God and celebrate life."

As I looked up and saw Joann's bright, sparkling eyes as she walked down the aisle, I was struck by my deep love for this woman. My mind flashed back to when we had first met, seven years earlier. "Wow, Lord. What a miracle You've done," I thought. "Not only in this community, but in my heart, too."

I could clearly remember the harsh, angry glare Joann had given me that first day as I walked by her house. I recalled thinking, "This is someone I will certainly avoid!"

And yet, over the years we spent as neighbors, God had brought us together, teaching us what it meant to love your neighbor—especially across racial and socio-economic barriers. He taught us how to respect, encourage, affirm, and love one another.

"What a gift Joann is to me," I thought. "What a special blessing for me today. I can't believe I'm privileged to be seated as the Mother-of-the-Bride!"

"Thank You, Lord, for the gift of this day and all it means, and for the gift of Joann's friendship. Thank You for giving me this special daughter."

I leaned over and whispered to Freddy, "This is probably the highlight of my ministry life in the inner city!"

The Hardest Time

The phone rang out in the darkness, startling us awake. I glanced at the bedside clock. It read 1:30 a.m.

"Hello," Freddy mumbled into the phone. Lying beside him, I could hear shrill screams coming from the receiver. Dread and adrenaline coursed through me. Frightened words and shrieks flowed from the speaker in a loud stream.

"Freddy! Oh my God, Freddy!" the voice cried. "Montrell has been shot! I think he's dead!"

"Oh no, Quenita! Oh no! How? Where? This can't be!" Freddy sat bolt upright, tears already on his cheeks, holding the receiver in disbelief. "I'll be right there."

A little while later, the phone rang again. Freddy told me through his tears that, yes, the life of this promising, precious young man of 19 had been lost to gun violence.

After I hung up, I sat in the darkness in utter disbelief. I sat as the memories of this precious young man flowed back to me.

I recalled our first encounter with 5-year-old Quenita and her 8-year-old brother, Montrell. Their rental house was three doors down from our home on E. Franklin Street. Soon after we moved in, I remember catching sight from our kitchen door of two figures chasing a ball into our backyard.

Freddy and I went outside and said, "Hi! We're the Johnsons. We're glad to meet you."

Later, Quenita recounted that meeting as well, saying, "You invited Montrell and me into your home that day. You were able to see outside our current situation into the vision God gave you for two little neighbor children. You put us together with Bob and Maggie Wynne through the ministry's big brother/big sister program. As our friendship grew over the years, we loved each other as family."

From that day forward, Montrell had been at Freddy's side almost constantly. Trips to McDonald's became frequent, and Freddy took Montrell on numerous fishing trips. The two would study God's word in our home weekly, and together they assembled bikes for our Pride for Parents Christmas Store. As their relationship deepened, Freddy even had visions of Montrell being the Director of BTM someday.

Montrell's loss was devastating. The grief that descended upon us that day would leave a large hole in our hearts for always.

* * *

Even as I still grieve for Montrell and the future we imagined for him, I also rejoice in what God has done in the life of his sister, Quenita. After Bob and Maggie Wynne moved to Montreat, North Carolina, in their retirement, Quenita joined them, finishing her degree in nursing while caring for Maggie in her final years.

Inner City Raleigh and Haiti Connection

The connection between Haiti and inner city Raleigh was present for us from the very beginning. It was a connection we nurtured. Ten percent of the early yard sales held on the baseball field at Peace College went to support children in Haiti. When we moved into the school building, the basement became a thrift store with ten percent of all proceeds continuing to be donated to Haitian causes. From early on, I envisioned that an important part of our ministry would be to organize trips to Haiti with interested folk from across Wake County joining neighbors from Halifax Court. We would call the trips *COME AND SEE*, and we would invite teams to see Jesus in Haiti in the midst of pain and hope.[17]

When the trips actually began to take place, some of the single mothers and grandmothers living in government housing traveled with our teams and upon returning home committed to support a Haitian child at $25 per month.

Virginia Bennett and her daughter Eva were two of the women who took a trip with us. Mrs. Bennett shared with me while in Haiti, after learning that most children in Haiti cannot afford school and must receive sponsorship: "I wish for all the world that my grandsons could just be here and see this. These youths in Haiti have almost nothing but the clothes on their backs. I can't get over how hungry they are to learn. Can you believe they stand as they study under the single streetlight of the compound! Our children don't know what they have. If only they had this hunger to learn. I will go home and send my little bit of cash each month to support one of these children. They are so worthy."

One of the other Halifax mothers wrote and shared from her journal: "When I'm there in Haiti, I experience a fresh form of prayer as I witness the children whose primary conversation to their Papa are exclamations of their trust, gratitude, and love for Him. No matter what comes their way—earthquakes, floods, hurricanes, kidnappings—not a cry of 'Where are you, God?' but instead, 'God, you are faithful. You are love. And mercy.'"

A Child's Faith

Young Jephte, a child Freddy and I sponsored, sits beside us on the rough benches of the church in Haiti, his head resting on the back of the pew in front of him. He is simply, quietly conversing with the God he knows is there with him. He makes simple statements of thanksgiving for who he knows God is.

The question I had to ask myself was "How do I stay tuned in to God like that, knowing His presence? How can I hold the pain and hope of the city together with trust like these children do?"

Holding Christ

Our pilgrimages to Haiti often included visits to Mother Teresa's Hospital in Port-au-Prince. On one of those visits, I overheard one of our team members ask one of the Sisters of Mercy as she beheld the rows of metal cribs filled with crying babies with fevers and runny noses, arms reaching up to be held, "Sister, do we need to be concerned that we might contract illnesses from the sick babies?"

I was embarrassed and whispered to the nun, "I'm sorry. I apologize for our insensitivity. Thank you for your patience. I hope we are not adding stress to the marvelous work you do here."

"Oh, no," she kindly responded. "You came to hold the babies. We believe that when you do so you are holding Christ himself. You came with the gift of your presence. Thank you!"

And so I returned to the city of Raleigh, North Carolina, having held pain and hope and little ones—and believing those little ones to be Jesus himself. What a privilege.

Haiti Lessons

Through the years I have learned that, in Haiti, presence means more than words. Even when you don't speak Creole, love can be communicated in so many other ways.

I think of Vivian, a 15-year-old girl, standing in front of me, frankly admiring my clothes. She reaches out and gently takes the scarf from my neck, wraps it stylishly around my head, stands back, and smiles. Eye contact, a mischievous sparkle, a wink, a bright laugh—I am embarrassed by her love-filled gaze. As we turn and begin walking down the rocky dirt road, she reaches over to remove a speck of dirt from my shoulder, a loose hair too—then her hand gently falls into mine. How much there is to say and yet no words are needed.

I think of Jephte, sitting next to me at the closing evening program, drawing my arm and hand tighter around his frail frame, wiping tears from his cheek with his free hand. He knows we are leaving the next day. He says without words, "I love you. I am sad to see you go. I will miss you."

And I think of gentle lips, soft kisses on my cheek, and strong lingering hugs from the women with cheek resting on cheek.

After each Haitian interlude, I return home with a fresh desire to share the love of Christ with my eyes, my touch—and with fewer words. Slowing down, being present—*really present*—to hear people's stories, being available and ready for the hug or the prayer that is needed in the moment, as when my neighbor Joann shares her dream of getting a job that would grant freedom from an unhealthy relationship.

Away with grocery list prayers. Instead, I strive to substitute everyday conversation, talking to Papa like Jephte did, naming all God's goodness. My desire is to simply express my gratitude for the gift of each day, for my family, for my neighbors, for God's presence, and for His love leading the way.

Haitian lives are filled with crisis. They are continually surrounded by pain and loss. Yet they rarely grumble, and they don't hurry. They calmly approach their path each day with a peaceful gait. Calendars and schedules carry little meaning. They walk with trust and live in gratitude.

Lord, help me to do the same!

Lessons From Betty

Betty Burdette clung to my hand as we quietly sat in the waiting area of Rex Hospital. Betty was a regular participant in the weekly women's Bible study at Halifax Court and a dear friend. Now we waited nervously for a report from her husband's doctor.

Finally, the doctor approached us. "I'm so sorry, Mrs. Burdette, but your husband just passed away. He went peacefully."

In a daze we barely heard the rest of the doctor's words. Then we walked together, Betty's grip on my hand even tighter now, to the hospital room where Ray lay. Tears streamed freely down her cheeks as she reached down to affectionately stroke the locks of hair on her husband's still head.

The holy moment was interrupted by worldly concerns. Betty turned to me, her cheeks glistening and her forehead wrinkling into a frown. "But," she stammered, "I only have fifteen dollars! How will I bury him? He doesn't even have a proper suit."

My sadness for Betty immediately turned to indignant anger at God. I thought, "Lord, the poor have so little. Can't they even be allowed the luxury of a few moments to grieve?"

As I battled with my angry thoughts and feelings, my friend interjected with a soft whisper. "The Lord will provide!"

"Yes. Yes, God will," I said. But to myself I thought, "Oh, sure God will! This is impossible! Funeral arrangements are so expensive. And where will money come from for Betty's other bills? Where?" I knew Ray had no insurance and no savings. And now Betty had said she had only fifteen dollars to her name!

Once again, God ignored my petty doubts. As the day progressed, I could only stand in awe as a witness to the ways the Lord provides for those who depend on Him, for those who know Him, for those who love Him.

God's first provision was a call from the Social Security office informing Betty that a check from a widow's fund in the amount of $250 would be mailed to her. The second provision came from benevolent friends at Brown-Wynne Funeral Home in Raleigh. They would handle all funeral arrangements for Ray, and the charge would be minimal. The amount quoted: $250!

God's provisions kept coming. Friends brought food. Checks showed up under Betty's doormat at Halifax Court. A donation came in for a suit, a white shirt, and a tie. Ray would have proper attire for his burial.

Yes, Betty, the Lord *will* provide. God does provide for His children who love Him and trust in Him. With God, nothing is impossible! Thank you, Betty, for continuing to teach me these kingdom lessons.

Needing Each Other

E ven a heartfelt "yes" to God's call to relocation and ministry in Raleigh's inner city did not bring immunity from the temptations of the world. They simply came in a more subtle disguise. I began realizing this as Freddy and I continued into our eighth year with Building Together.

National, state, and local recognition, a growing staff, accountability to faithful supporters, and the acquisition of the NeighborCenter, though all clearly blessings of God's grace, had become for me a new place of struggle. The recognition, growth, and heightened sense of responsibility produced pride, a desire for control, and compulsive busyness, instead of humble gratitude and dependence on God. As I succumbed to these temptations of ministry, I became increasingly diverted from God's original call to minister His love by simply loving Him and loving my neighbor.

As God revealed this truth to me, I decided to let go of my board and administrative duties. I began letting go of anything and everything apart from our original call of building relationships. As soon as I did so, my joy began to return, along with renewed strength.

During this time, someone asked me what my greatest joy over the previous year had been. I was surprised by my response: "My greatest joy has been spending time with our neighbor and my dear friend from Halifax Court, Carolyn." Joy hadn't come with awards or with the ministry's growth or even with the ownership of our beloved old building, the former Barbee School. Instead, joy had come in the simple gift of sharing God's love with a friend.

For years, I had wanted to teach crafts to our neighbors to help them discover their gifts and encourage them toward a degree of economic independence. Over the previous few months, a small group had met, prayed, and dreamed together. We had decided to establish a craft group called Gifted Hands. We received commitments from several local businesses to sell art produced by Gifted Hands.

When the scheduled time for the first class arrived, not one woman showed up. I returned home discouraged and confused. Had I truly responded to God's voice, or was this just another "Helen Thing"? But in faith I scheduled a second class and waited.

As I arrived in the Gifted Hands room for the second class, I found my friend Carolyn sitting alone.

"I started not to come," she said with downcast eyes. "It's really a down time for me."

She was, I suppose, surprised when I confessed, "I'm a little down myself."

I was certainly wishing that more neighbors had turned out for Gifted Hands. But then, as we began to talk and paint some old furniture and gift bags, Carolyn brightened. She explained to me how she had wanted for years to order a course by mail that promised to teach her to paint.

"But I didn't have the $40, and even if I did, how could I even hope for a place to sell my work," she said, knowing I'd see the futility of such foolishness. "Now, though, there's a place to learn, and I might be able to sell my gift bags at Logan's or at the bakery in Cameron Village. It's a dream come true!"

As we worked together, we did as women commonly do; we shared our hearts. There were quiet words of encouragement. I reminded her how far she had come and what she had accomplished and what a witness of perseverance she was to me. At the end of the day, we held hands and prayed together. Tears flowed as we found ourselves in the Father's loving presence.

As we prayed, I felt the Father rekindle once again the love He had put in my heart years before for the people of this community. The doubt and confusion cleared. Gifted Hands was not Helen's thing. It was a God thing.

My greatest joy that year? Rediscovering the mystery and the miracle of God's presence. It had nothing to do with the numbers game; it happened quietly, in that hidden place where God's children touch and pray and encourage each other with hearts of love.

When we come together to receive from each other, vulnerable enough to be transparent, not in a place of strength but of weakness, God acts. And what He does for Carolyn, He does for Helen as well.

It Takes a Village

In 1994, after eight years in ministry, we were close to burnout. God's perfect timing intervened once again. We received notice that we had been awarded a six-month sabbatical through a grant from the Z. Smith Reynolds Foundation. We were two of the four recipients in the state of North Carolina, winning in the category of "Community Change." The award was designed to recognize individuals who, despite limited resources, had brought about significant change to a North Carolina community.

"Breathe…," I said to myself as I firmly gripped the podium at UNC's George Watts Hill Alumni Center in Chapel Hill. I was preparing to deliver words of thanks as we officially received The Nancy Susan Reynolds Award for Community Change. "This is not the time for tears or displays of emotion."

Looking out at the audience, my eyes connected with the many faces that had made this award a reality—our family who had sacrificed by letting us go, the neighbors who had received us, the committed staff of Building Together Ministries, the volunteers who gave hours of service and love, and the many who so generously supported our work financially. All of these people needed to be standing in this place. I was overwhelmed with gratitude.

"We believe that there is great hope for our inner cities. Community change begins small, almost invisibly, with a smile, with an encouraging word. We thank God for His call on our lives, for our journey to the inner city of Raleigh, and especially, for His heart of love for His people in the city."

I'm thinking to myself, "We're most grateful to have been given the 'gospel of neighboring' as a guiding force in our lives, which has meant helping, sharing, caring, understanding, committing, and realizing that all people have gifts and resources, tangible and intangible. We learned that we are not saviors trying to 'save' Halifax Court, but rather friends and neighbors trying to listen and to help."

"Lord, thank You," I prayed silently as I looked into the audience. "Your presence was manifested in all those You sent to do Your work in downtown Raleigh! Thank You!"

From Doing to Being

As we backed out of the driveway in early June in our used RV— The Special—I was ready. Our long-anticipated sabbatical lay ahead! Cupboards and refrigerator were stocked; our menu box with new crock-pot recipes was full; stamps, postcards, stationery, and address book had been gathered; hiking equipment and rain gear had been packed; and, most important of all, my tote bags were brimming over with reading and writing materials. Our mini-library included travel guides like *Fodor's Canada* and *Alaska Off the Beaten Path*, devotionals, novels, three Bible translations, and five empty journals. I was ready and eager to receive all that God had in store for us in this gift of extended Sabbath time. In my heart I was prepared to glean from each and every experience, asking God at each turn, "What's Your message for us in this, Lord?"

At our campsite the first evening, I felt like a child again, playing house as I prepared dinner in my tiny RV kitchen with my new "tea sets." What fun! For our first dinner, I enthusiastically decorated the rough picnic table outside our door, spreading it with a new lavender plastic tablecloth. On top I placed royal blue candles, two stemmed Lucite goblets, matching blue-and-lavender plastic plates, and flatware. I had even brought royal blue cloth napkins. Such a beautiful table setting for two. Had she ventured by, Martha Stewart would have been proud of my spread!

The gourmet romaine salad was topped with roasted walnuts, tiny bits of crumbled blue cheese, and balsamic vinaigrette. Freshly grated parmesan cheese was sprinkled atop the mounds of hot spaghetti and sauce. It was so... romantic!

"Wow!" Freddy exclaimed with genuine pleasure. He quietly lit the blue candles.

Then, in unison, we both sat down close together on the picnic table's attached bench.

To our utter surprise, in one swift movement, we found ourselves flipped over onto our backs in the mud of our campsite. We were covered in hot spaghetti, walnuts, and blue cheese, pinned under the heavy picnic table. In our excitement and anticipation, we had failed to observe that the picnic table had not been level. By sitting together on the lower side, our combined weight had tilted the whole thing over!

For the longest time we just lay there laughing—then laughing some more.

"What's God's lesson in this?" I joked, gasping for air. "Reckon it has something to do with balance?"

"Yeah," Freddy replied. "Like maybe we've been too one-sided!"

As we cleaned up the mess, we continued to talk about the importance of balancing work and play and time alone with God. Maybe God was letting us know from the start of this sabbatical that He was giving us the chance to learn to play more, to spend time in quiet with each other and with Him.

"I'm ready to learn," Freddy said. "How 'bout you?"

And so, for most of the six months away, we saw no one we knew (except when Ashley and three grandchildren joined us for a week at the Grand Canyon). It was Freddy, me, and our Lord. We immersed ourselves in His creation. We visited national parks and hiked numerous breathtaking mountains. We slept and rested and ate fresh vegetables and fruits from local markets. We cooked special chicken recipes in the crock-pot. We spent time in silence as we hiked and were surrounded by God's cathedrals of giant trees.

During this time of renewal, two quotes spoke to us especially. The first was from Oswald Chambers, who wrote: "The greatest competitor of devotion to Jesus is work done for Him."[18] The second came from Paula D'Arcy: "There is nothing inherently sacred about an act of service. It can bless you or lead you astray. My eyes had been filled with acts of service and God was now saying to me, You have no room for Me... I do not create time to be with HIM. My life has had no stillness and no space. My life has no silence."[19]

As we wrapped up our sabbatical, we prayed from grateful hearts: "God, we are ready—and so very thankful for what we've learned in just being *with You*. We understand the need to *be* before we *do*. This will be a new priority."

For the remaining years we were given together, Freddy and I faithfully set aside time to simply be with God and each other, at first quarterly at Mepkin Abbey, a retreat center in Moncks Corner, South Carolina, and then later at St. Francis Springs Prayer Center in Stoneville, North Carolina. Over the years, during our retreats at The Springs, Freddy designed walking trails that were added to the features of the prayer center.

Not Again

"Not again!" Freddy shouted to me as we entered the auditorium to prepare for an event. The soaking wet carpet in the middle of the room revealed another irksome leak in the roof.

Freddy and I had retired from BTM in 2005, but we remained in the community and still lived in our home on E. Franklin Street, continuing with "the gospel of neighboring." Freddy stayed connected to the NeighborCenter with a part-time job maintaining the grounds and being on call for crises.[20]

"I guess you'll have to call Prentiss again!" I said.

After multiple visits over 12 plus years to repair roof leaks, Prentiss Baker, owner of Baker Roofing Company, finally said to Freddy, "This roof has really been beyond repair for years. We've found ways to patch it up so far but, Freddy, it is getting to be too hazardous for our workers to get up there and make repairs. The roof deck has deteriorated so much as to make it a dangerous situation for anyone who gets on the roof. I'm sorry. Really sorry. But we've done all we can."

After this news, the BTM staff gathered among the strategically placed metal buckets in the auditorium to pray. Our prayers for help we offered to our most reliable provider—the Lord! "God, You know we don't have the finances to replace this roof. You know our need. HELP!"

Within a few weeks of our saying this prayer, God began to show us his answer. Broadcasters from ABC notified BTM staffer Linda Hawkins Riggins that her family's home was being considered for ABC's renovation series *Extreme Home Makeover*. The house was located on Poplar Street directly behind the old Barbee school building where Linda worked. Linda invited us as her coworkers and friends to participate in the pre-production interview.

We met for the scheduled interview on a rainy Sunday morning. Everyone gathered on the Rigginses' front porch. We shared about our relationship with Linda and pointed out the school building across the street where we worked together.

"Tell me more about the work you all do at the school," the reporter prompted.

Concerned that the conversation was straying from Linda, I quickly answered, "We really don't need to focus on the old school building right now. I think our focus should be on Linda and her family's needs!"

"But, Mrs. Johnson," the reporter interrupted. "You don't understand. *Extreme Home Makeover* has enough resources to rebuild the Riggins home and renovate Linda's workplace too. We can do both!"

And so, on the morning of November 30, 2006, the familiar *Extreme Home Makeover* bus rolled down Poplar Street in Raleigh, with full police escort, announcing that the Riggins home and Building Together Ministries would both receive an EXTREME MAKEOVER!

What an amazing answer from our Provider, our Creator, to the specific need we had brought before Him in prayer among the buckets—a new roof!

The "C" Word

A new interruption of our spiritual journey came in 2013 when we heard these frightening words: "Mr. Johnson, I'm sorry to report that you have stage 4 prostate cancer."

As I heard these words spoken by a urologist, my heart filled with panic and dread. I tried to listen to what the doctor was saying, but instead I found myself thinking of a quote from Anne Lamott's *Help, Thanks, Wow: The Three Essential Prayers*: "Most of us figure out by a certain age—some of us later than others—that life unspools in cycles, some lovely, some painful, but in no predictable order. So you could have lovely, painful, and painful again.... Awful stuff happens and beautiful stuff happens, and it's all a part of the big picture."[21]

Sitting beside my vigorous, seemingly healthy husband, I silently cried out to God. "God, I need some beautiful stuff in the midst of this awful stuff! PLEASE! With this unsettling news, You are taking us to another place we would not choose to go. Please show us the way. You are our provider for health and finances. Have mercy! Please help with this new interruption in our lives!"

Freddy had an aggressive form of prostate cancer. The "c" word forced us into a state of urgent decision-making. We sought advice from family members and friends and settled on Duke University Medical Center for Freddy's care. Its location close by in Durham was an added benefit.

The doctors at Duke recommended immediate removal of the prostate. Surgery was scheduled and successfully performed. Follow-up tests six weeks later revealed, however, that cancer had been detected in one of Freddy's lymph nodes. When we shared this news with a doctor friend, his response was far from encouraging.

"Man, that's not good, Freddy. This means the cancer has metastasized!"

It was time for a second opinion. My sister Jane recommended M.D. Anderson Cancer Center in Houston. We flew to Texas, where a specialist recommended radiation treatment. "But to be really honest, we won't know our target. There's only a 20% success rate for this procedure here."

"And so God, where do we go from here?" we prayed.

The next step came from a phone call with our friend George Turner.

"Fred, you know I had the exact problem you are facing," said George. "Sue researched and researched, and we decided to go with the Dattoli Cancer Center in Sarasota, Florida. They seemed to have the best cure rate. With Dattoli's special imaging, the doctors can detect the exact size and location of the metastasized prostate cancer cells. They also use a specialized Dart Radiation Technique. I think this is your answer. Praise God, I have been cancer free for six years."

Taking George's advice, we made a trip to Sarasota in early 2014 to check out the Cancer Center and to look at rental possibilities. If we decided on Dattoli, Freddy would be beginning his treatment in March, in the middle of "snowbird season." We soon discovered that rentals were scarce and very expensive.

"Well, we are at the end of our list," I said, feeling tired and hopeless. "I feel like we've come to a dead-end."

"Then we'd best pray before we go into this last possibility," Freddy whispered to me.

Entering the manager's office of a small motel on the beach, Freddy said, "Good afternoon. My name is Freddy Johnson, and this is my tired wife, Helen. We've spent hours looking for rental space for 10 weeks beginning in March. You are our last resource!"

"Glad to meet you! My name is Linda," she said with a welcoming smile.

"Linda, we are from North Carolina, and we're not here for vacation. We'll be coming to fight cancer. We have limited resources, and a rental here would carry us beyond budget. Do you possibly know of other, cheaper rentals in Sarasota?"

Linda thought for a moment and then said, "I believe I know the perfect place! A good friend of mine is also fighting a rare cancer and will be traveling to Venezuela for treatment. Her small house is in a simple neighborhood within walking distance of the Dattoli Center. She would like to rent her home when she goes for treatment. Let me make a call. This could be a win-win situation!"

As Linda made the phone call and explained the situation to her friend, Freddy and I held hands and said another one of our "HELP!" prayers.

When Linda hung up, she said, "Carol said this sounds like a plan, for you and for her. She would love to meet you at her house at three o'clock this afternoon. If that works for you, I'd like to give you a parking pass for the beach. Parking for the beach is a major problem here."

God had answered our prayer in a manner far better than we had imagined. He had found us an affordable home plus a beach parking pass to boot! We left Sarasota confident in the care Freddy would receive at the Dattoli Cancer Center and grateful for the home in which we would reside for the 10-week stay.

The Road to Healing

As Freddy backed the car out of the driveway for our trip to Sarasota in February of 2014, I sat in the passenger seat tallying up some last-minute checks, cash, and gift cards from friends and family that had arrived in the mail or that we'd found tucked under our front doormat. In awe and with thanksgiving I saw that the total of the gifts was the exact amount for our precalculated budget—$3,600. An added bonus gift was a fabulous Vitamix we could use to make healthy smoothies.

"God is good!" I said, turning to Freddy with a smile. He replied with a response we heard frequently from our neighbors, "All the time!"

The day we arrived in Sarasota, our neighbor, Janet, was the first to greet and welcome us. She stood at our front door leaning on her cane and balancing a bag of Meyer lemons from her backyard. She was to be the face of God for us during our 10-week stay on Martin Street. Janet was 87 years old, a retired high school teacher and a widow of five years. Janet held the ugly stuff and the beautiful stuff, as God would have all of us do. The ugly stuff involved grief, neuropathy, vertigo, and macular degeneration. The lovely stuff was her joy for life, her hospitality, and her positive attitude. "The doctor told me to stop ironing because standing still was not good for my neuropathy. So I hired Janice to iron for me, and I went outside and cut the grass."

God had provided the perfect place for treatment and recovery. Freddy's radiation was scheduled daily at 9:00 a.m. The procedure took approximately 20 minutes. The rest of the day was open for adventure, healthy food from a local Amish market, tennis for Freddy at a local recreation park, walks to town, worship at a local Mennonite Church, exercise at the neighborhood YMCA, restful trips to the beach with our books, and time to meet our neighbors.

Our rental home provided space for visits from our children and grandchildren. Freddy remained hopeful and positive, making friends with others in the waiting room at Dattoli, players on the local tennis courts, and all who crossed his path, including his doctors.

When the time came to celebrate Freddy's last radiation treatment, Janet invited us to her home for dinner. As we entered, she ushered us to the dining room and pointed to the end of the table where three place settings were ready. The other end of the table was covered with stacks of old magazines, mail, and photographs of her late husband, Rog. The dinner she had planned, shopped for, and cooked was a veritable feast. Each item had been carefully selected from Freddy's list of favorites.

I thought about all that had gone into this gift. This precious neighbor who barely knew us had driven at daybreak, before the traffic, to hand pick each vegetable that was roasted. She'd gone to the fish market for fresh shrimp from the Gulf. The spread included roasted whole garlic cloves, homemade tartar sauce, mango sorbet, her favorite wine, and beautiful light pink orchids. A feast full of thought and love!

As I once heard Paula D'Arcy say at a retreat, "The magic is not in putting a plate in front of someone, it's in how you put it down, the love with which you do it."

May I always be reminded of this quote as I feast with family and friends, as I eat and drink, sitting around talking and telling stories and cleaning up after the last bits of the meal. May I remember what Jesus said to his friends at dinner, "Whenever you do this, do it for the remembrance of me." And may I always say *Thanks* and *Wow*!

It is not that I am happy for the suffering Freddy went through. Who would be, who could be? But I am happy for the new level of intimacy with the Lord to which the suffering brought me.

The light and love of Jesus surrounded us. We were carried! My initial cry of "God, You know You are carrying me to a place I do not wish to go" changed to "Thank You, God. Wow, thank You for this journey!" What a glorious adventure!

After 44 radiation treatments, Datolli declared Freddy "clean." Not cured, but clean. On his final visit, he was privileged to sign Dattoli's survivors' wall, a wall covered with signatures of men from all over the world. Thanks be to God!

A Wind of Holy Change

In 2018, Freddy was diagnosed with myelodysplastic syndrome (MDS)—preleukemia. Less than two years later, the nation experienced the onset of the COVID-19 pandemic. During this time, God showed us a phrase in Pamela Hawkins' book *The Awkward Season*: "I will lean into the wind of holy change." This came to be our mantra as we journeyed into the year 2020. And change did indeed sweep in as a strong wind. It blew away the comfort of life that we'd known for 80 years. We experienced a major setback in our retirement income.

When we had retired from Building Together Ministries in 2005, part of our retirement budget came from Freddy's job maintaining the grounds and yard of the BTM property that he knew so well. His role continued even after the property had been taken over by a charter school called Hope Leadership Academy. He loved cutting the grass, maintaining the landscaping, and being on call for crisis events.

When HLA closed, the decision was made to sell the property. The new owners—The Fletcher Foundation—were unsurprisingly no longer interested in Freddy's services. And so, we began to seek options to make up for this retirement budget loss.

Once again, God provided in a wondrous, amazing way through generous, benevolent saints. Freddy's sweet sister Kate and our dear brother-in-law Tommy Fonville found a way to help with our retirement budget. They bought a brand-new, energy efficient home in the new community of Wendell Falls in Wendell, North Carolina, just 18 minutes from Raleigh. The home is in their name, but we were given living rights to this gift until we passed.

Little did we know when we moved in, but our time as a couple in our beautiful new space would be a brief six months. We moved in on January 19, 2020, and Freddy died in hospice, as was his choice, on July 19. Can I lean into the wind of this holy change? Can I face this loss and emerge in a larger place? So many questions remain as I determine to move forward.

"I cannot change what has happened but I can change how I live. What is, is! I don't want any days of my life to slip by unlived. This grief is like a searchlight uncovering hidden things.... I'm fighting to keep my heart open in spite of the emptiness and tears. And LIFE is right here, patiently waiting for me to look in its direction." –Paula D'Arcy[22]

One of God's Fishermen

Freddy's memorial service was held at Hayes Barton United Methodist Church in Raleigh. Due to the restrictions in place during the COVID-19 pandemic, we were allowed a maximum attendance of 20 family members. I invited our family to write letters to Dad, Papa, Freddy. Four family members were designated readers—our grandson, Ross Bell; our daughter, Ashley Bell; our granddaughter, Sarah Johnson; and our brother-in-law, Tommy Fonville. In the middle of the worship center, lit by candles, my great-grandfather's tacklebox, which Freddy loved, was festooned with greenery and with antique lures dangling from small twigs. As the service closed, our family walked to the foot of the arrangement and gently placed their letters at the foot of the box. Our pastor, Rick Clayton, said, "This arrangement is a symbolic representation of who Freddy was. Freddy was gentle in spirit, vibrant with light and love, with a keen eye for the living color of people. He cast a net that embraced everyone. He was one of God's top fishermen!"

The letter to Freddy from our grandson Ross:

Dear Papa,

Not that I did anything special to deserve it, but I feel so fortunate that as your first grandchild I got to spend just a little bit more time with you than the other grandchildren. (Sorry, cousins). As I was recounting memory after memory I have with you, I realized that of all of my memories it seems that the ones with you are the richest and most vivid. For example, thinking back to my life as a six-year-old, I truly don't remember much but I keep coming back to one memory of the two of us on the sand at Wrightsville Beach, watching you blow up this inflatable boogie board in like, three breaths, and then being terrified in my mind as I looked out to the ocean as a storm approached and seeing massive waves that were way too big for any human to tackle, let alone a child without a life jacket. I also remember having the time of my life and feeling safe, feeling invincible knowing that you weren't going to let anything happen to me, and that I could live in that moment truly free without fear.

It seems like for every year of my life, 28 of them now, I have a memory like this of you, where you are Mr. Rogers from Mr. Rogers' Neighborhood and I think in a lot of ways I saw you as my real-life version of him. There was always a lesson to be learned, but instead of sitting me down to explain right and wrong, you taught by example, treating each situation and each person with intrigue and understanding. Except I saw you more like a Mr. Rogers on steroids, or like a hybrid of Mr. Rogers and James Bond. I mean, how many grandfathers can whoop your butt in tennis in the morning, do a double backflip off the diving board after lunch and then help a family in need by bringing them a heavy load of furniture in the afternoon. Granted, lunch did probably take two hours to get down (or "savor" as you liked to call it) so you had plenty of time to rest up.

Switching gears to more recent years, I have been so lucky to have been able to spend the last six years or so in Raleigh where I have been able to trade my "technical expertise" for a home-cooked Nana meal and a long sit-down with my two favorite people on the planet. Luckily Nana doesn't really retain anything technical, so I'll have plenty of opportunities to spend lots of time with her.

I always knew how unique and special you were as a grandfather and as a person, but it's really come to light for me over the past year as our country seems more divided, politically and socially, than ever before. I know it has pained you to observe everything that's going on and I'm not going to pretend to have any answers for what should or shouldn't happen, but what I'm convinced of is that I can at least do my part by trying to live my life with you in mind as much as possible. Be more selfless, without quick judgments, live life with less shame and embarrassment, have more fun, ask myself in tough situations or faced with a fork in the road, "What would Papa do?"

By doing these things, I can only hope that when I get to my end, I can achieve what your last wish was for me when we said our goodbyes, which was to be able to go knowing that I've live a fulfilling life with no regrets where my relationships and memories will live on forever in a positive light.

Love,

Ross

Words shared by our granddaughter Sarah:

There are people in your life that are always constant. You know they will always be there. You know that they love you. He was just there. He was at every major life event I had.

If I had to choose a memory that was first, it would be at sleepovers at Nana and Papa's. You see, going to Nana and Papa's was always my favorite time. They lived in a cute cottage in downtown Raleigh. Maybe the reason my brother KJ and I loved it so much was there was a huge Krispy Kreme two blocks from their house. We knew that Papa loved to get up early, and Papa was always up for a good walk, especially to Krispy Kreme. As we walked there, he would laugh with us, tell us some good stories and always say hello to every person he passed.

As I got older, I began to realize Papa was an adventurous one. While he would tell you "I am just one man," he would try to do just about anything that just one man probably shouldn't do. He would drive us around on 4-wheelers, take us skiing and tubing, toss footballs and frisbees to us in the yard, go snowmobiling (breaking Nana's ankle accidentally), hammer the tennis ball on the court to us. I found a picture of all the grandkids out in our pond in inner tubes and lifejackets. I broke down and cried because up until a month ago, Papa still had that same energy. In the picture, he was right in the middle, building relationships with us.

If you had told me in March at our cousin's dinner, this would be the last time I got to hug my Papa, I would have said, "You are crazy!" Papa had always been the healthy one. The one making trails with his bare hands. To be honest, I'm not sure how to deal with it all. I am thankful he isn't in pain anymore. My heart aches because I loved him dearly. So, Papa, your "Country Girl" misses you. Praise God you gave your life to Him. Thank you for not just being a grandfather, but a grandfather that was there in the midst of it all with us. Your legacy will live on in us. I look forward to the day when we are reunited once again in heaven. It was a good ride!

Papa, thank you for living it to the fullest, pedal to the metal... wholeheartedly loving everyone you came in contact with.

Love,

Sarah

Pastor Clayton asked me to close the service. I began with a poem Freddy had requested to be included in the program at his memorial celebration.

TAKE THE TIME

Take the time to sing a song
for all those people who don't belong
for the women wasted by defeat,
the men condemned to walk the street
the down and out we'll never meet.
Take the time to say a prayer
for all those people who face despair:
the starving multitudes who pray
to make it through another day,
who watch their children slip away.
Take the time to hear the plea
of every desperate refugee:
the millions who have had to flee
their lands, their loves, their liberty,
who turn in hope to you and me.
Take the time to take a stand
for peace and justice in every land
where power causes deep unrest.
Come, take the part of the oppressed,
and then, says God, you will be blessed.

–Miriam Therese Winter (1987 Medical Mission Sisters)

I concluded with the story of a phone call I had received that morning from a dear neighbor and friend of ours, Juanita Taylor. For years Freddy and our friend Craig Herb had used Freddy's old open-back white truck to make deliveries for The Neighborhood Network, a food security program under Juanita's leadership. On the call, Juanita said, "Helen, I was praying this morning. I said, 'God, You sent that beautiful, loving, kind, caring angel Freddy here for us, to help us in our time of need. I guess now You want him back. Thank You, God, for THE LOAN of Freddy to us!'"

Our "Go-To Place"

I knew that my place to grieve after the last of the family had left following Freddy's funeral was our "Go-To Place," St. Francis Springs Prayer Center in Stoneville. As I was packing for my planned three-day retreat, I reached into a large plastic bin in our walk-in closet and grabbed one of Freddy's journals, paying no attention to the year in which it was written. I stuffed it into my backpack with my Bible, my own journal, and Paula D'Arcy's books *Rivers of Sorrow, Currents of Hope* and *Seeking with All My Heart*.

I soon settled into my favorite spot at the retreat center, in the library—a room filled with books by African American authors. It was good to just *be*. In the quiet, I read and prayed and listened. On the second day, the director—Steve Swayne—joined me, and we shared stories of Freddy and his love for the prayer center and the surrounding beauty of God's creation in nature. Freddy had called it his sanctuary.

Steve said, "Father Louis and I know how he loved being here at Saint Francis and how the two of you would come often to experience the presence of the Spirit in the quiet of this place. And he was instrumental in creating the trails."

Freddy had indeed spent hours walking through the forest on the grounds. And God had given him a vision for creating trails through the forest he loved. He had approached Father Louis Canino, the founder of the prayer center, with plans and an offer to help construct the trails. The plan had been accepted, and trails had been constructed.

"So, with your permission," Steve continued, "we'd like to dedicate the trails to Freddy's memory by naming them FREDDY JOHNSON'S TRAILS."

My heart resonated with this request. "Freddy would be honored, I'm sure."

"Your assignment," Steve said as he stood to leave the room, "is to choose the words for the plaque!"

As I went to bed that same evening, I prayed, "Lord, how do I show a life of 80 years so well lived in four short lines? I think I need some help!"

During the night, the name of a dear friend came to mind. Byron McMillan had been part of a men's discipleship group Freddy had put together many years ago. Byron likes to describe himself as "just a boy from Carolina, growing into the reality that we all belong to each other and are trying to communicate as best we can."

So the next day I placed a call to Byron, who was now living in New Mexico.

"Byron, I really need your help. St. Francis wants to dedicate their walking trails in Freddy's honor. Would you please share your gift of writing and come up with a few words for the inscription to be engraved on the marker?"

The very next day, Byron sent these words: "Freddy Johnson quietly blazed trails of wisdom, humor, love, life and dirt everywhere he went. He beckoned us all to follow not just with words but by his deeds. Enjoy God's presence and the Oneness Freddy discovered on these trails."

Reading these perfect words brought to mind the piece Byron had written in his blog *Riverflow* at the time of Freddy's passing:

A MAN OF GOOD TROUBLE

Freddy and Helen Johnson began encouraging me to do this bridge-building work many years ago. My heart is heavy today with the news of his passing back home in Raleigh on July 19.

Freddy was a bridge-builder and knew how to get into good trouble. He understood the travails of this work and his main strategy was to build beautiful and enduring relationships. Freddy knew that getting into good trouble is only possible with good friends.

When I worked with folks to bring the Christian Community Development Association (CCDA) to Raleigh in 2014, people said, you have to get Helen and Freddy on board if you're going to make it happen. Freddy and Helen befriended me and made my life better. They sent me on a weekend retreat to relax and rejuvenate at St. Francis Springs Prayer Center near my birthplace in Greensboro, NC.

Freddy is the first person who told me about the men's work of Illuman and affirmed the work I was beginning with Richard Rohr and the Center for Action and Contemplation.

They hosted dinners with the incomparable John Perkins and invited me to attend.

Monthly, Freddy sent out poetry, readings and other bits of wisdom to a few men who had gathered together for years to inspire and motivate each other to be positive masculine forces within our communities. Here is one of the last bursts of wisdom he sent to us: "I discovered a gem at the end of Rohr's daily meditation this morning I feel like sharing: 'Love what God sees in you.'"

He lived it by looking in the mirror every day and he lived it by seeing in you what God sees.

Freddy, my friend, you will be missed greatly.

God's Faithfulness Even unto Death

Nearing the close of my time at St. Francis, I began to read from Freddy's journal that I had randomly selected and brought with me. In those pages written twelve years earlier I found God's gift to me in my deep grief—a clear sign of His faithfulness to Freddy and thus to me. Written in Freddy's handwriting on July 21, 2008, were these prayerful words: "Prepare me for death, that I may not die after long affliction or suddenly, but after a short illness with no confusion or disorder, and a quiet discharge in peace with adieu to brethren."[23]

Our gracious God had honored his request in every way. Freddy was still playing pickleball three weeks before the Myelodysplastic Syndrome developed into full-blown leukemia. His illness had been short. He was of sound mind to choose hospice care. He was at peace and ready to die. He was able to say goodbye to family and friends and to enjoy his last mocha frappé from McDonald's.

Underneath his prayer in the journal, I found a second request: "I pray I don't outlive my body (usefulness)."

I sat in amazement at God's faithfulness. God had honored my husband's prayers down to his last request.

Another Angel

Returning to our newly built home that we had enjoyed for just six months together, I became aware that my grief was lapsing into depression. Everything reminded me of Freddy's absence. The beautiful handcrafted raw-edge table he'd found in a consignment store stood in the dining room. The fire screen art piece he had discovered at Ten Thousand Villages, the maker-to-market fair trade store, stretched across the hearth. His favorite spot on the screened-in back porch, where he meditated each morning before sunrise. The empty antique desk chair in his study.

I prayed once again, "God, help me navigate this path of grief. Help!"

During this tough time, I found a bit of relief by taking the 18-mile trip into Raleigh multiple times each week. I would pop in on a friend, stop by the church, or do a bit of shopping. On one of these ordinary days, I bumped into my potter friend Gretchen Quinn.

"Hi, Helen! I've been thinking about you a lot during this time of loss," she said. Then, after a pause, she added, "Can you keep a secret?"

"Sure," I responded, my curiosity rising.

"I'm moving my studio from Boylan Heights to Five Points at the end of the month!"

"I'm so happy for you, Gretchen! What a great location."

"And...," she continued dramatically, "I have space for you!"

Thoughts swirled in my head. Having space in a professional studio to work on my pottery would of course be a dream come true, but I knew I didn't have the resources to pay for my share of the expenses in such an upscale location.

"That's so kind of you," I replied, "but with Freddy's death I'm on a bit of a limited budget."

"But... you don't understand," said Gretchen with a soft smile. "I just want your presence."

I stared at her blankly.

She reached into her purse and slowly drew something out. "Here's your own key. Come whenever you can."

God knew that—as I walked my path of grief—putting my hands in clay would be part of my healing. Having a place to go that was away from the house would give me renewed purpose. And I would be able to create once again, grieving and healing as I did. What a blessing!

God's Beloved Community

O n Saturday, November 27, 2021, family and friends gathered to celebrate Freddy's life and dedicate the walking trails Freddy designed and laid at St. Francis Springs Prayer Center. All of God's people— young and old; rich and poor; black and white; Republican and Democrat; conservative and liberal; believer and non-believer—gathered to tell stories; to worship, pray, and sing; and to laugh and share tears.

Father Louis Canino, the founder and visionary of the prayer center, began the morning with prayers and a scripture reading in the quiet of the out-of-doors that Freddy loved so much. With his usual touch of humor, Father Louis told of Freddy approaching him with his first thoughts of the trails.

Our voices rang out in joy as we sang *Shine Jesus Shine* and *Guide My Feet, Lord*. Byron McMillan spoke about the message he had written for the plaque at the head of FREDDY JOHNSON'S TRAILS. Then Duane Beck, our retired Raleigh Mennonite pastor, neighbor, and good friend, shared Freddy's personal mission statement, which I had discovered after his death.[24]

Each person in attendance was given small pebbles to drop on the pathway as we walked from the labyrinth to the trailhead, where Father Louis dedicated and blessed Freddy's trails.

Following lunch, David and Rosene Rohrer sang a song David had written when BTM began in 1990, entitled *Neighborhood*. After this, several people—Keith Johnson, Barry Parker, Mauricio and Christina Chenlo, Rick Clayton, John Drescher, Mary Burr Edwards, Diana Allen, and Linda Riggins—shared stories of Freddy's life. Our lifelong friend Chuck Millsaps, adorned in Freddy's favorite white felt cowboy hat, strummed his guitar as he sang the country song *The Older I Get*.

I was the last to speak. I reminded everyone that Freddy and Senator John Lewis had died two days apart, and I closed our time together with Senator Lewis's words: *"One hundred years from now, I would love to see that our*

Beloved Community, the place we call home—America—will be more at peace with itself. Let us hope and believe that there will be less turmoil, less rancor, less violence. America should be a place of respect and dignity, a beacon of light for all of our fellow human beings. I know it is within our power to make such a world exist. Be patient. Be hopeful. Be humble. Be bold. Be better. Keep the faith. CARRY ON."[25]

I said, "It's not just the John Lewises or the Freddy Johnsons, but it is for all of us to *be* and *do*."

I want the end result of having known and loved Freddy to be the creation of more love in me. –Helen Johnson

Faithful to His Promises

We began our journey by pondering God's questions and then through scriptures that spoke to our souls. In the beginning, God promised, "Truly I tell you, there is no one who has left houses… or father or mother or children for my sake… who will not receive a hundredfold more in this age."

I realize now in 2023 that God is faithful to his promises. Freddy and I have family in downtown Raleigh, in Haiti, in Atlanta, and in Wendell—a hundred-fold. The very best part of answering His question to us—*Would you follow Me?*—is humbly receiving His tender whisper to our hearts, "Thank you for following, and thank you for loving Me."

And so, I join Freddy's joyful statement from his ICU bed: "It's been a good ride, Hon!"

The Final Chapter Is Love

Freddy not only taught me how to live but he showed me how to die.

I recall as he was gently transported from the ambulance into the quiet hospice facility, he exclaimed, "Oh my, this is amazing!" Freddy personally knew two of the doctors who had founded this remarkable place of peace and care. His mind and heart immediately went from self to others. As he lay in bed, he asked for his handy, pocket-sized Day-Timer. He smiled as he found his doctor friends' names. Contact was made, and Freddy was able to express his gratitude to them for their vision and the gift of this place in which he would spend his final moments. In his dying, there was no fear, only a heart of love and gratitude.

I read somewhere that as long as a person has a dream in their heart, they cannot lose the significance of being.

Even in his final days, Freddy was dreaming and planning what the new pickleball shirts for Hayes Barton United Methodist Church would look like. He drew several designs on a small piece of paper from his cherished, thoroughly worn-out Day-Timer. He held up the small design for me to judge.

"What do you think? Should these words be on a curve or printed in a straight line?"

A dream coming true! Pickleball shirts from church for a game he had come to love. A game where folk were given the opportunity to know one another, to become a community, to teach others what LOVE and FUN look like.

His strong physical body knew life for 11 days in hospice. Our granddaughter Emma flew in from a Navy base in California. Due to COVID rules, we had to sneak her into his room. In the quiet of the hospice room, Keith and his daughter sat on either side of his motionless body, his eyes closed.

"Dad, Emma is here," Keith said softly.

Without words, with eyes still closed, Freddy gently took hold of Emma's hand and raised it to his lips for his last kiss.

Friends and family and those we have yet to meet, *love what God sees in you!*

Freddy dearly loved you all.

All Along It Was YOU!

Paula D'Arcy writes in her book *Seeking With All My Heart*, "C.S. Lewis is believed to have said of God, 'So it was You all along.'" She follows with: "So, it was You all along. It was Your exquisite timing. It was You in every human contact, every event.... You, standing beside me on the highway when the drunk driver hit our car.... You, holding me when I buried my family."[26]

And I'd like to add my own list:

So, it was You all along.

You, saving Kent's life through open-heart surgery.

You, handing us Foster's *Freedom of Simplicity* to simplify our life.

You, calling us to surrender our lives on that North Carolina beach and at Windy Gap.

You, with constant divine interruptions inviting us to Come and See You on the holy ground of Atlanta, inner-city Raleigh, and Haiti.

You, teaching us the *gospel of neighboring* in Atlanta and in Raleigh.

You, providing HELP and provision for the mothers of Halifax Court who cried out, "Help us help our children!"

You, in every staff member, every volunteer, every financial contribution, every neighbor at Building Together.

You, beside us through COVID, cancer, and leukemia.

You, holding me as I witnessed Freddy's ashes poured into the soil.

All along, it was You.

ALL ALONG, it was You!

Epilogue

Divine Interruptions

Laura Kirby

Divine Interruptions. Sometimes they creep in quietly, like a small voice in the night. Other times we might glimpse a Divine vision or have a fleeting thought and know there is a different way. But we always have to be attuned and listening. The Johnsons have modeled this deep listening, this deep noticing, this deep awareness of the Spirit moving in their lives. To stop, to start, to move, to rest… in the pages of this book we witness faithful responses to God's nudging in their lives. In the words of Pastor David Beam, "God seems to specialize in disrupting people's lives. God specializes in taking all our expectations and predictions and turning them upside down and inside out."[27]

The Bible offers us story after story of Divine Interruptions. Noah, Abraham and Sarah, Job, Jonah, Mary, the list goes on and on. Pastor Beam proposes that "you could argue that every character in the Bible is interrupted in some way by God. Because if your name is in the Bible, it means that at some point God showed up in your life and disrupted what you were doing."

Catholic Priest and Theologian Henri Nouwen said, "I have always been complaining that my work was constantly interrupted; then I realized that the interruptions were my work."[28] Helen and Freddy made it their lives' work to listen and respond to Divine Interruptions. Their lives were a life of faith where they were constantly preparing their souls to follow an unpredictable God. As reflected in the pages of this book, we do not know the day, the time, or the place when we will hear God's voice. We cannot anticipate "when grace will burst into [our] lives—but when it does, Jesus says it will always take you someplace new." Into the heat of Haiti, the heart of downtown Atlanta, the holy ground of Halifax Court, and the peace of

Wendell Falls… the Johnsons have listened, have trusted, have moved, and have followed… and have shown us all that life will never ever be the same.

Photo Collection

First date, 1953

Wedding Day, June 23, 1961

Kent, Keith, Ashley

The Johnson Family, 1968

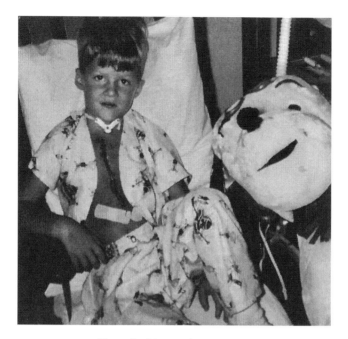

Kent after his open-heart surgery

Family on steps of the Ridge Road house in Raleigh

Wrightsville Beach—enjoying simplified life

Wrightsville Beach—sister Jane, Ashley, Helen, and mother Clara

Helen, Ashley, Freddy—grateful smiles

Ashley and Tim's wedding reception, June 1987

"Can't you just picture us looking out over this peaceful, gorgeous view of Haiti?"
I asked Freddy.

Saying our good-byes—Mom and me as I leave for our new home in Haiti, July 1987

Mwen grangou! I'm hungry!

Freddy at Sunday worship (photo taken from our upstairs room)

Albert Schweitzer Hospital—even the latex gloves were washed and reused

A home in Haiti

Next-door neighbor Tammy and family building their home in Atlanta

Bob and Maggie Wynne visiting our Ormond Street home in Atlanta

John Perkins in Jackson, Mississippi—1987

John Perkins with team in Jackson

Getting the house in shape—Helen, sister Jane, and neighbor Latoya Carney

The house on E. Franklin Street, Raleigh

Peggy Dublin, Halifax Court Resident President, with Barbara Steadman on a BTM outing

Roderick Steadman, the first youth in the Friends Program

Preparing for a fundraising yard sale

Bob Wynne with Chris, Sissy, and Quenita

Let's go camping—Friends Program Director Stan Wiebe

Friends Program kids at Camp Sea Gull

Friends discover new adventures outside the city

Praying together at Kids Across America, Branson, Missouri

Friends Program trip to New York Youth Conference

Kids in the Sing, Spell, Read, Write Program with Carolyn Coley Koning

Durk Steed with friends from Sing, Spell, Read, Write

Gifted Hands Program participant and friend Carolyn Tyson with her daughters

Freddy and Montrell assembling bicycles for the Pride for Parents Christmas Sale

Johnny Evans and family bringing gifts for the Pride for Parents Christmas Sale

Our son Kent selling trees and poinsettias at the Pride for Parents Christmas Sale

Hands-on relationship building with Carol Sloan, BTM Board Chair

Linda and Helen with Chris and Sissy in our backyard Bible Study

Latesha McCullers Greene helping blind neighbors Janice and Wallace Brame with groceries

Neighbor Joann's wedding party

BTM staff Skip and Andrea Long teaching swimming

Getting cool during BTM Summer Camp at the NeighborCenter

Adopt-a-Grandparent crew boating on Lake Gaston

Neighbor Johnny with pet parakeet

Andi Clark and family, with her mentor and friend Anna Neal Blanchard

Kathy Boos' Growing Together Preschool offers love to kids like Keyshaun

Delores Steele Richardson and Carol Worth

Quenita Winston and Maggie Wynne, lifetime friends

Family time in Montana—Kate Fonville, Helen, Freddy, Keith, Shelly, and Tommy Fonville

Vacation time at Wrightsville Beach with grandson Ross

Answered prayers—a new roof!

Duane Beck, Freddy, and Anne Cooper enjoying the festivities associated with
ABC's *Extreme Home Makeover*

Sabbatical trip—Death Valley and Alaska

Sabbatical trip—Ashley, Ross, Andy, and Emma joining us at the Grand Canyon

Freddy and Helen with their sponsored youth, Gary and Lubens

Freddy with John François and his family

Classrooms

School lunch—maybe the only meal for the day

Freddy teaching

Brenda Herb with student

Haiti team from Building Together and Halifax Court

Wash Day

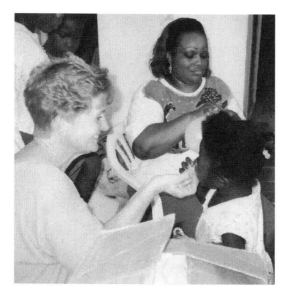

Helen and Reggie in Haiti

Andrea Long with friends

Sue Turner with children in Pacot, Haiti

Kelly McInnes Swanson visiting one of our Haitian partner schools

Father and son with father and son in Tin Village, Haiti

Raleigh women's team to Haiti, 2012
Back row: JoAnna, Melanie, Adrienne, Kim, Helen, Pat, Lindsay
Front row: Suzanne, Mary, Bev, Anna Dunn, June

Baby goat and friends bring a smile

John François and the beginnings of his church

Tracy Hawkins with a precious bundle

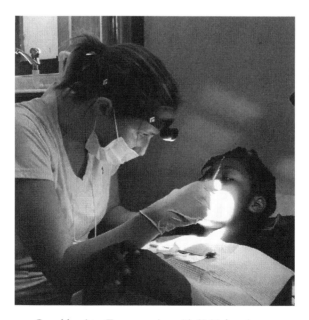

Granddaughter Emma serving with Haiti dental team

Ashley and Yodendy—Mother/Daughter Trip, 2013

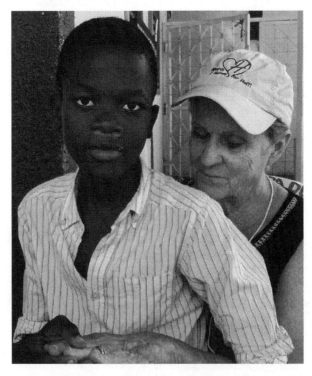

Departure brings gestures of love for Helen and Jephte

Joyful smiles despite challenging circumstances

Pickleball to celebrate Freddy's 80th birthday—Helen, Sara Chenlo,
Myrtle Allen Ward, Mauricio Chenlo, and Linda Riggins

Wings Book Club at E. Franklin Street—Susan Cook, Alice Fowler, Bettie Murchison,
Carrie Alspaugh, Anna Neal Blanchard, Donna Seligson, Anne Cooper, Lindsay Newsome,
Joanne Barnes, Deborah Wright, Lucy Allen, Helen Johnson, Reggie Edwards

From Raleigh to Alabama for the Women Speak Conference with Paula D'Arcy—
Willie Parker, Reggie Edwards, Pat McInnes, Helen Johnson, Anissa Ferris, Brenda Millar,
Marsha Smitley, Lacrecia Daniels

Keith, Ashley, Kent

Blessed with six grandchildren—Andy, KJ, Ross, Ben, Emma, Sarah

Family

Granddaughter Sarah brings joy and fun

Adventure-loving grandson Andy taking a rest during a Grand Canyon hike

Grandson KJ—another fisherman in the family

Family gathering to celebrate grandson Ben's graduation from the Kansas City Art Institute

Sold!

Freddy in his "quiet time" chair in the midst of COVID and MDS

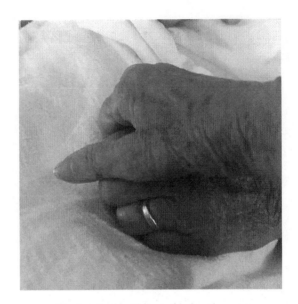

Hands joined until the end in hospice care

Ministry History

Feeding the 5,000

Deanna Drescher

The site of Building Together Ministries, the old Barbee Elementary School on Blount Street, has a history of twists and turns. It began as part of the Pilot Mill community, one of the first developments in Raleigh. Workers in the old Pilot Cotton Mill were housed in the community and, as the population grew, a school was needed. Barbee School was built in 1924 to educate the white children of Pilot Mill. This remained as the neighborhood school until the 1970s. The white flight of the 1950s through the 1970s, coupled with integration woes, led to the closing of Barbee School in 1976. Wake County Public Schools used the site for an alternative school for a while but that, too, closed. The Pilot Mill community sat on valuable land that was increasing in value with each year that passed. The mill neighborhood, houses and mill buildings, were razed around 1982, and only a few buildings were left standing, including the Barbee School building. This four-acre property, owned by the Wake County Public School System, became the headquarters of Building Together Ministries in 1991 for the enormous rent of $1.00 per year.

As Building Together grew into its mission with more and more community partnerships, the Blount Street site served as the base of outreach. As years passed, Building Together continued to establish a firm footing in the community, and supporters saw the benefit to purchasing the site in the early 1990s. For $327,000, the old Barbee School building and land, a place that at one time had excluded some of God's children, was purchased to keep opening its arms wide to a community that included everyone. The building and grounds were overseen by a Board of Directors under the umbrella of Building for Hope, Inc. In the by-laws, any future profits from the sale of the building and property could only go to nonprofit organizations that benefitted children and families living in poverty. The recipients of the funds would be chosen by the directors of Building for Hope.

In 2001, the main floor of the building was leased to a new charter school appropriately named Hope Elementary Charter School. Hope Elementary served the surrounding, now more urban, community until 2018 when it closed. What would be the greatest use of this property now that the school was gone? When one door closes, another opens.

In 2020, The Fletcher School expressed interest in the campus to house their lower school grades. The Fletcher School's mission says that it "is committed to helping unique learners flourish and achieve to their fullest human potential by teaching indispensable academic, artistic, athletic, social, and technical skills for life." Building for Hope agreed to sell the property and buildings for over two million dollars, as the location on which it sat had vastly increased in value over the years. In the lobby of the Fletcher School lower school campus is a quote from Freddy: "We couldn't feel better about Fletcher School carrying on in that building. I'm so impressed with what their mission is, what they are going to do with that building. And you know, they are going to take it over the top of anything we could have done."

Once the site of Building Together and Hope Elementary was sold, the board of Building for Hope remembered their mission. The profits from the sale of the property were to be distributed among organizations serving those in poverty.

In the Gospel story of Jesus feeding the multitudes of people, his disciples ask him if they need to go and find more food. Jesus answers by asking them "How much do you have? Go and see."

Building for Hope's answer: We have over two million dollars. We started with $1 rent per year, and then with $327,000 we purchased the land and building.

Then Jesus commands his disciples to divide what they have, once He blesses the food, among those gathered. Feed them, He says. A small amount, five loaves and two fish, feeds them all.

The loaves and fishes were multiplied and divided by the Board of Building for Hope. Over two million dollars went into the community.

East Wake Leadership Academy, the Southeast Raleigh YMCA, Camp Sea Gull, Triangle FCA, Greater Pleasant Grove Development Corporation,

Your CenterPeace, Note in the Pocket, Hope Reins, The Green Chair Project, ROAR, PAVE, Growing Together Preschool, Young Life, The Encouraging Place, Hearts and Hands for Haiti, Raleigh Mennonite Church, and Focus Raleigh were among the recipients of the funds.[29]

What had started as a small ministry was multiplied and divided by God's grace. Where we saw challenges, God saw opportunities to be in community. Where we saw small obstacles, God saw big ways to help. We had loaves and fishes, and God gave us a bountiful supply to be shared 30 years later among the people in our community. In the story of the feeding of the 5,000, we see that Jesus didn't just meet the minimum needs of the people, he supplied them with overflowing amounts of food. He gives us much more than we could ever imagine. He used his disciples to distribute the food, and they grew to depend upon and trust Him even more. We are blessed that our community was willing to receive God's supply and in turn, bless others with what they were given. Although Freddy was talking about the Fletcher School buying the property, maybe he also knew that this ministry had blessed others in a big way, long after it started. "And you know, they are going to take it over the top of anything we could have done."

Loaves and fishes....

Other Voices

In the body of this book, you have heard God's story in our lives through my voice. The following section will allow you to hear the voices of other characters in the story. These testimonials—solicited and unsolicited—come from those who served alongside us, both staff and volunteers, and from the neighbors among whom we served.

Maggie Wynne

For several years, I had the joyful assignment of interviewing and writing about staff members, neighbors, and volunteers at Building Together. If there was any one consistent theme that sounded in the lives of those I met with, it was this:

"It feels like family here. I sense God's presence in this place."

Putting these words together I was reminded of the essay "Birthing Compassion" by Sue Monk Kidd, an eloquent Christian writer. In it, she pursues the meaning of true Christian community. She calls it "the community of the Compassionate We."

As I focused on the stories of volunteer families, I heard many reflections like those above. I came to realize that it was just such a community that God brought into being at Building Together, and I rejoice at the privilege of having been a part of it.

Virginia Bennett

We volunteers became like a family.

It all began with a chance conversation I had with Helen Johnson as she was walking the streets of Halifax years ago, getting to know her new neighbors. I was raking leaves in the yard when Helen came by, and she expressed the need for someone to help sort the mountains of clothes that were accumulating in storage as people began to hear about Building Together and make donations.

I agreed to help. After that, my relationship with the ministry deepened with each passing year. The humble beginnings of what would later become the NeighborStore started with community yard sales of clothing and household items. My daughters and I were among the volunteers who staffed the sales at the Peace College ball field.

I still remember my first Pride for Parents Christmas Store in 1990. It was held in Stan Wiebe's little white house down the street from the college. I remember moving into the NeighborCenter the next year. I remember beginning to operate the NeighborStore year-round and the excitement of acquiring hangers, and at last, real clothes racks for the store!

We worked together as a family—Betty Bickel, Carolyn Lees, Judy Millar, and, of course, Stan. We worked hard, but we had fun together too. Eating breakfast out together. Sharing a meal at my house. Praying for each other.

My own family became very involved as well. Eva served on the board and had a paid position in the store. Linda was actually the first member of the Bennett clan to volunteer, inspired by one of the ministry's early trips to Voice of Calvary in Jackson, Mississippi. My youngest son, Jeff, became a "regular" in the store. And my grandchildren—Randy, Michael, Larry, Janene, Daniel, and Michelle—all either participated in the programs of the ministry or volunteered, or both.

Roderick Steadham

One of my many memorable moments about Building Together was when I first met Freddy Johnson. I was in the seventh or eighth grade, playing football for Daniels Middle School. Freddy told me he would come to one of my games. About a week later we had an away game and, while on the field playing, I looked up toward the sideline and there was Freddy standing with our supporters a few feet from the team bench. That really meant a great deal to me. Fast forward about two or three years and I'm working at Camp Sea Gull for the summer. Freddy comes down for a visit and gives me a book by Dr. Ben Carson. The title was *Think Big*. As a teenager I didn't get it, but as an adult I totally get it, and that's the message I would preach to the kids I've coached and mentored. I still have the book 30 years later.

Andi Clark

I'd like to take some time here and talk about a program whose effects on my life are endless. The summer before middle school was a landmark summer for me. It was my first summer in the neighborhood and my first summer camp experience, where I learned how to play tennis and where I met my future partner in the Friends Program—Anna Neal Blanchard. At the time, she was the summer camp tennis coach, and she saw something different in me from across the net. That following school year we became partners through the Friends Program. This is a program that pairs adult mentors with kids like me and gives them an added personal and positive influence in their lives. The spunk of that red-headed kid was matched by the determination and love of Anna Neal to help me reach my potential. We've shared everything, from clothes, a house, tears and laughs, and a love for ACC basketball. The Building Together family, with their values and their love, has inspired me to be so much more than I could have ever imagined myself to be. And for that, I am forever thankful.

Diana Allen

First, giving honor to God, who is the head of my life.

I came to North Carolina to attend a wedding, but little did I know that God was about to change my life forever through Helen and Freddy Johnson. You touched my heart in such an amazing way. I was broken, had low self-esteem, and no trust. You opened many doors for me that I had only dreamed about. You moved into a community to enhance and change that community, but before you can change the community you have to change the people in the community, and that's what you guys did with Building Together Ministries.

You offered me the opportunity to travel to Haiti, to Wilmington, NC, and to Montgomery and Mobile, Alabama, as well as participating in a small craft business program called Gifted Hands. (Diana hand painted a donated bedroom suit to pay for her first month's rent in an apartment.)

That's just a small portion of the journeys I traveled with you.

Freddy, you were an amazing man, and you touched the hearts of so many. But can't nobody tell my story like I can. You taught me to believe in myself. You taught me to never say what I could not do. Today, I carry that with me. I'm doing amazing things from what you taught me. I got my first car when I got to North Carolina and my driver's license. I got my first home. But most of all, I got unconditional love from you and Helen, and for that I will be forever grateful. I thank God for your family, sharing such an amazing man with me. You have earned your crown. Wear it well. Your chocolate daughter, Diana Allen (Her words at Freddy's celebration of life)

Quenita Winston

Maggie and Bob created a long-lasting, quality friendship made from unconditional love, selflessness, and empathy wrapped in compassion for all of God's children. I was the blessed recipient.

Freddy encouraged me to keep going toward my nursing degree every time he would visit Montreat. Well, I made it.

My love and passion for nursing is constantly evolving and growing, but the one thing that remains the same is the happiness I feel when I am at the bedside, caring for the aging population. I absolutely love my profession, and I don't know another career I'd rather have!

Thank you, Wynnes and Johnsons, for listening to the still, small voice that said, "Move into My troubled neighborhood and help these families with the true heart of servant leaders."

E. Patrick Walker II, SGT, US Army

Growing up I think it would be safe to say that I was a troubled teen. I've always heard about the great potential I possessed, but we all know what they say about idle hands. In an effort to keep me busy and out of trouble, my mother found a program for teens (Tuned in Youth sponsored by Building Together Ministries) that focused on educating youth about the dangers of smoking, drugs, and alcohol via public service announcements.

Ms. Dawnn Breynae, a BTM staff member, became very instrumental in my life, whether she was helping me overcome my fear of heights, teaching me how to write a storyboard, or encouraging me to reach that potential I had been hearing so much about. At such a critical moment in my life, I am grateful for the Tuned in Youth program at BTM and particularly Ms. Dawnn Breynae.

Latesha McCullers Greene[30]

Latesha, one of our 11th grade youth, wrote this poem after attending a Christian Community Development Association Conference with the Building Together community:

Making A Difference

Determined to stand up and try to make a difference.
Influencing some, if not all, but I continue to
Flee the devil, but staying on the ball,
Faith is what we need and what will get us through, but
Everlasting life is the gift so let God use you.
Running for Jesus is great, 'cause one day you'll see the Pearly Gates.
Everyone can make a difference or a small change,
No one will be rejected, 'cause we can all praise God's name.
Concentrate and call God's name,
Everyone can make a difference, we can make a change.

Jason Bobbitt

Long before I became known as Chef Mike on Tyler Perry's *Love Thy Neighbor*, I was "the kid who does wonders" in the Halifax Court housing projects of Raleigh.

It feels amazing to reflect upon going from those humble beginnings to great opportunities. Just knowing that a lot of people can't make it out, being trapped by their circumstances, having no idea that they can make it out. So, it feels great, and I feel humbled and blessed. Coming from the housing projects, where you are confined to being only familiar with the surroundings, to this Big World with so many dreams and aspirations. I feel like everything that I'm doing right now is up because I came from the bottom and came from nothing. So, that's kind of like how I reflect on coming from the projects of Raleigh.

One of my influences growing up in Halifax Court was the Building Together youth program, where they took kids growing up in poverty and gave them a positive role model known as a "partner," who would be their mentor. The Building Together program was one of my biggest positive influences.

Annie Singletary

I was a single parent blessed to get an apartment in the Halifax Court Community. While living in the community, it did not take long to realize that I was very much outside of my comfort zone. Daily I witnessed fights and negative activities from my bedroom window. These activities were not what I was used to seeing growing up. I favored communicating with my elders versus people more my age. One day I ran into Freddy Johnson, who happened to be walking through the neighborhood. While we were conversing, I shared that my daughter would start kindergarten soon. He informed me that she could participate in the half-day preschool program called Growing Together, which was held right in the community. I felt this program was a great opportunity for her. Who knew that this was the beginning of my getting acquainted with Building Together Ministries?

In 1997, the Executive Director, Delores Steele, asked me to consider coming to work at the ministry. I accepted the dual position as her assistant during the first part of the day and helping with the middle grades after-school program in the afternoon, which was great for me.

Building Together realized that a school was needed to continue assisting the children in the neighborhood. Working at the school really opened my eyes to what a lot of the students experienced in their day-to-day lives in the neighborhood. It was normal for staff to walk through the neighborhood and check on absent students. The home visits enlightened me. They also allowed me to make some very close friendships. Through visits with parents, I realized that just as I had a passion for my daughter to learn, so did they. We may not have run our homes the same, and the love and values for our children were not displayed in the same fashion, but we had a common goal—we wanted the best for our children.

Working at the ministry and school allowed me to step out of my comfort zone to allow Christ to use me to provide the best service that I could to all that I encountered. Despite what the situation looked like, I was able to dismiss preconceived thoughts that hindered me from seeing the beauty within. I will be forever grateful for the 20 years that I served families at Building Together Ministries and Hope Elementary.

Andrea Long

Every day became a treasure hunt, an exercise that proved beauty and purpose were found in the least likely of places but were as priceless as a crown of jewels. Helen was a master at taking an object, situation, or most beautifully a person and finding that hidden gem. Helen and Freddy together truly provided an opportunity for a collective effort in revealing museum-worthy works of art through smiles and laughter, work and play, and shared meals, coming together as neighbors supporting one another through challenges, celebrating in triumphs, and simply living life together.

My husband, Skip, and I had just pulled up in front of our house to find a precious nine-year-old little girl sitting on our front steps (I never found out how long she had been sitting there). She was a child in our after-school program and summer day camp. As we opened the car to remove the car seat cradling our newborn son (we were just coming home from the hospital), she just sat on the steps beaming. In her hands she cradled a gift for our son. She had gone to Building Together's NeighborStore and gotten our son a gift! Needless to say, I still have that little yellow onesie with the blue embroidery, and that precious child would come to live with us just two months later, becoming a part of our family for the next nine years.

I see Freddy taking twice as long to cut the grass because he would stop and speak to every person walking by, taking pure delight in shining a light on someone's day to remind them that they are what is important! You learn to welcome constant interruptions with grace because you have the privilege to empower someone with dignity and value. Yes, there were programs and activities at Building Together Ministries, but the bottom line, the desire to be salt and light, to give hospitality, came bursting through from knowing how much God's love gave life to us, and we didn't want ANYONE to miss that same love in their lives. Building Together was building *life* together.

Anna Neal Blanchard

In 1991, I started volunteering a couple of hours a week at Building Together Ministries in their after-school computer lab for children in Halifax Court. I had heard about Freddy and Helen and the work they were doing, and I wanted to help out. Two hours a week with delightful kids was a nice change of pace from my stressful job as a civil litigation attorney. I also believed that Building Together was doing just what Christians should be doing—helping and empowering folks on the margins of our society—by first responding to their "felt needs." Every week, I looked forward to working with the kids during a strict two-hour window.

One afternoon, Helen told me (in what I later found out was her usual MO) that she had a very specific need that she thought I could help her with. She explained that they were going to take a large group of kids to Camp Seafarer at the coast that weekend and that they needed one more adult to help with one particularly needy child. Could I possibly go—tomorrow? My immediate thought was "No way I'm giving up a weekend; this is not what I signed up for." I really didn't want to be gone for 48 hours with a bunch of people I didn't know and sleep in a cabin with a challenging child. But Helen was so earnest and so convincing that I wouldn't regret it, that I reluctantly said yes, if she couldn't find anyone else.

Long story short, within the year I quit my job with the law firm and set up an office at Building Together, providing legal services to neighbors in need while also working on a counseling degree at N.C. State University. Within two years, I was working as BTM's full-time Development Director, raising awareness of and funds for the ministry throughout Raleigh. It was a winding path to a job I loved but would never have chosen for myself without God's nudging and Freddy and Helen's mentoring.

Kathy Boos

I first heard about Building Together Ministries in the mid-1990s when the Johnsons shared their story at my church, Raleigh Mennonite. Their story and passion inspired me to volunteer as a tutor at Building Together's after-school program for children living in Halifax Court. Three years later, in the spring of 1998, I felt God's "pull" leading me in a new professional teaching direction that would bring me into a deeper relationship with this ministry. I met with Freddy, and plans were made to start a preschool program for community children. A large grant had just been received for such a program.

It was truly a God-inspired moment for me to witness doors being opened. Hearing God's call, I jumped at the opportunity and have never looked back!

We enrolled children for preschool in August of 1998, thus beginning my journey, my passion, and my joy of teaching and preparing young children with very limited experiences for success in kindergarten. I enthusiastically continue today creating smiles and joyful spirits of my two-, three-, and four-year-olds at Growing Together Preschool.

Warren Keyes

My title was Director of the Skip Long Computer Center. The hope was that the kids who came to the after-school program, most of whom did not have computers in their classrooms, would be exposed to computers and a computer-based learning environment. I was also there to be a role model for the children, allowing them to see an African American male in an authority role, one of leadership, stability, and a loving Christian bearing. We were, to some degree, successful, and, in one instance, highly successful. I speak specifically of one of our computer center students who later would become a computer support person for the State of North Carolina Legislature, who spoke of the computer lab as an inspiration for her career in computer support.

I saw God moving in many ways during my time at BTM. Being present when a city child sees the ocean for the first time, or seeing people of means give freely to folks who have so little. I witnessed people working hard to reconcile racially, though there is no handbook or guide on how to do this. I saw God in the faces of Freddy and Helen when they, with open arms, invited folks from the neighborhood to come and be friends. God moved my heart much closer to poor people and people who just couldn't seem to catch a break in life.

My BTM experience allowed God to open my heart and mind, which increased my understanding of the difficulties and weightiness of poverty and the generational pull that poverty exerts. I am bolder to speak on behalf of poor people and to exert some effort to help. BTM brought home the impact of being aware and considerate of others' life situations, and BTM helped me be a more mature follower of Christ.

Brenda Millar

Through seminars and visiting speakers, I was exposed to the plight of racism in my all-white college experience. In the working world, I had contacts with black adults and taught black children. But it was through my friends Helen and Freddy and their work at Building Together that I began to be exposed to situations where I could be involved in action with people of color! My heart and soul have been deeply touched by the opportunities to grow in being a part of understanding and finding solutions to racism.

Helen Collier

In order for us to reflect on anything, we have to get far enough away to look back at it. That is when perspective is added to dreams and visions. In the bright light of perspective, we can see learning and growth in new ways. As I reflect on the beginning of Hope Elementary School, I see how many different groups and communities came together to talk about blended visions of how Hope Elementary could look and serve its students and parents. Our first motto was *Changing the World One Child at a Time*. Much work and shared effort and prayer had already created resources we could use to "wrap around" and support each student and their shared community. I feel so blessed to have been a part of this beginning. I learned so much from the people with whom I was blessed to share this experience. When I reflect, I see commitment and effort from many people, and I remember changes and growth in many individual Hope Elementary students. God's love and His will built bridges of HOPE that will continue to connect and proclaim that GOD IS LOVE!

Gratefully, Helen Collier, First Principal of Hope Elementary School

Acknowledgments

I'm extremely grateful to Margot Starbuck, my extraordinary writing coach, for taking on an 83-year-old in the throes of grief, who was committed to fulfilling a promise to her deceased soulmate. Margot's constant encouragement and guidance were just the ingredients needed for me to stay on track. I also feel awe in having found Paul Koning—such an insightful and gifted editor—who polished my thoughts and words, and who also did much of the book design and formatting. And where would I have been without my friend Brenda Herb, who put the manuscript into its correct place. She was so patient with my illiterate computer knowledge. Together, we shared tears and laughter as the text was built. There are no words to convey my gratitude to these three. Also, very special thanks for gifted ghost writers: Laura Kirby, Paul Koning, Deanna Drescher, Kim Millsaps, and Maggie Wynne. Truly The Divine put together this team for HIS story.

Through prayer and interest in my writing project, this group of encouragers has kept me on track: June Chidlaw Adamio, Diana Allen, Karen Augustin, Arlene Bagwell, Sally Bates, Kay Barnett, David Beam, Holly Beasley, Anna Neal Blanchard, Robert Boone, Kathy Boos, Emily and Tom Bowers, Dorothy Bowman, Cheryl Burgess, Father Louis Canino, Mary Clayton, Rick Clayton, Andy, Sara, and Mauricio Chenlo, Anne and Dave Cooper, Melanie and Ken Crockett, Paula D'Arcy, John and Deanna Drescher, Mary Burr Edwards, Reggie Edwards, Mae Esposito, Anissa Ferris, Ben Fischer, Josh and Paige Fisher, Kate and Tommy Fonville, Andy Fowler, Linda Hargrove, Brenda and Craig Herb, Henri and Teddy Hoffman, David Horner, Patty Hunt, Carey and Janey Hunter, Father David Hyman, Laura Kirby, Vicky Langley, Andrea Long, Bob Lupton, Tim and Joy Matuse, Jerry and Pat McInnes, Byron McMillan, Brenda Millar, Anna Dunn Miller, Kim and Chuck Millsaps, Lindsay Newsome, Frances Morisey, Bettie and James Murchison, Nancy Nutt, Pam and Greg O'Connor, John Ormond, Lanny Parker, John Perkins, Bob Pearson, Gretchen Quinn, Sandra Rawlings, Pat

Reed, Chris Rice, Delores Steele Richardson, Linda Riggins, Paula Rinehart, Jennifer Schaafsma, Robert and Donna Seligson, Kim and Graham Shirley, Lina and John Siebert, Marsha Smitley, Tammy Summers, Steve Swayne, Sue and George Turner, Myrtle Allen Ward, Janice Waterman, Stan and Patty Wiebe, Tricia Wilson, Quenita Winston, Cathy Wooten, and Bob Wynne.

I am also deeply grateful for the love and support of my family: Keith and Shelly Johnson, Ashley and Tim Bell, Kent and Pam Johnson, Emma and Andrew Wood, Ben Johnson and Mollie Caffey, Andy Bell and Erin Funk, Ross and Allison Bell, Sarah and Evan Hill, KJ Johnson, Jane Neblett, Kate and Tommy Fonville, Mary Burr and Val Edwards, Anna Dunn and John Miller.

I read somewhere that God does not call us because we have great gifts, talents, or wisdom. He doesn't need perfection. He only asks for willingness—a willingness to be used. And when we show up, He can be counted on to enable us to fulfill the task.

The following names are just a few of those He sent to provide prayers, countless hours of volunteer labor, financial resources, and all the talents, wisdom, love, and kindness needed for HIS WORK. Freddy and I are deeply grateful for all those listed and not listed who gave their LIGHT to this community. (After our retirement in 2005, nearly all Building Together Ministries records, photos, and newsletters were destroyed. If you were involved and are not listed here, please accept my apology. All of you were valued and were gifts to the community.)

BTM staff and volunteers:
June Chidlaw Adamio, Diana Allen, Tiany Allen, Jim Anthony, Susan Anthony, Bo and Judy Batchelder, Carol Beaumont, Janet Bell, Sheri Bedsole, Ashley and Tim Bell, Andy and Ross Bell, Marilyn and John Bender, Jeff, Linda, Michelle, and Virginia Bennett, Bette and Don Bickel, Janelle Bitikofer, Cathy Birkey,

Anna Neal Blanchard, Sarah and Robert Boone, Kathy Boos, Rosie Boston, Erin Kesterson Bowers, Wallace and Janice Brame, Jim Branch, Sally Breedlove, Dawnn Breynae, Jim and Sharon Bright, Ruth Brooks, Jackie Bullock, Pam and Lee Bunn, Betty Burdette, Suzanne Burger, Ellen Byrum, Carolyn Carruth, Dorathy Chance, Vicky Chapman, Mary and Jack Clayton, Tina Clyburn, Joan Coley, Helen Collier, Elizabeth and John Converse, Anne and Dave Cooper, Lamont Cooper, Cathy and Alan Creedy, Yolanda Darden, Sandra and Lawrence Davis, Melinda Delahoyde, Calvin Denson, Steve and Barbara Derthick, Mildred and C.A. Dillon, Jessie Dingle, Tommy Drake, Peggy Dublin, Scott Earp, Kathy Eash, Cathy Ector, Reggie Edwards, Joan Elliot, Jennifer and Ralph Ennis, Sarah Ennis, Johnny Evans Family, Anissa Ferris, Janet and Todd Fields, Tommy and Kate Fonville, Richard and Emily Fountain, Joyce Fox, Jonathan Friesen, Addie Gatewood, Connally Gilliam, Felicia Gillis, Robbie Graham, Latesha McCullers Greene, Arlene Griffis, Linda and Charles Gupton, Dione Hall, Marcella Hamilton, Alice Hancock, Linda and Claude Hargrove, Nancy Harris, Cathy Hawkins, Tina Hawkins, Tracy Hawkins, Brenda and Craig Herb, Margie and A.T. Herring, Susie and Kevin Hershberger, Jeanette Hicks, Betty and Carlos High, Carey Hill, Elizabeth Hogan, Kriston Hoist, Diane and Eddie Jackson, Keith and Shelly Johnson, Kent and Pam Johnson, Wilbert Johnson, Mariechen and Joe Johnston, Elizabeth Jones, Warren Keyes, Ruffin King, Carolyn Coley Koning, Rick and Judy Lacks, Don Layton, Carolyn Lees, Mary Litzinger, Robert Logan, Skip, Andrea, and Matthew Long, Donna and Monty Mantey, Ruth Ann Marenyi Family, Sarah Marks, Fraley Connell Marshall, Elaine and Bob Martin, Horace Mason, Sriprakash Mayasandra, Beth and Lewis McMillan, Joanna and Doug McMillan, Knox McMillan, David McNeill, Paul and Judy Millar, Leah and Brenda Millar, Stacy Miller, Bonnie and Lowell Miller, Angeline and Bill Mills, Chuck and Kim Millsaps, Frances and Johnny Morisey, Jane Neblett, Stan and Brenda North Martin, Barbara Orthner, Mabel Pace, Willie and Barry Parker, Susan Parrish, Sister Mary Pat, Sally Plyler, Gary Preston, Natalie and Bill Prewitt, Shenita Rawls, Al and Ruth Reberg, Cathy Reese, Richard Reuben, Liz Rice, Delores Steele Richardson, Linda Hawkins Riggins, Paula and Stacy Rinehart Family, Martha and Franklin Roberts, Ann and Jim Robinson, Rosene and David Rohrer, Phyllis Ross, Kelly and Pete Ruhl, Salisbury Family, Eddie Sartin, Karin Shank, Annie Singletary, Ruth and

Joe Sipple, Temple and Carol Sloan, Shirley Smith, Roderick Steadman, Durk Steed, Tammy Summers, Kelly McInnes Swanson, Nancy Swope, Morgan Taylor, Vincent Terry, Richard and Davina Thrash, Richard Tilley, Cheryl Thomas, Eva Clinding Tucker, George and Sue Turner, EsDorn Westbrook, Patty and Stan Wiebe, Elizabeth Williams, John and Barbara Wilson, Mike and Frances Worsham, Carol Worth, Wanda Worrell, Maggie and Bob Wynne, Shana Zambone, Anastasia Judge and others at Underwood Elementary, Service Adventure Groups, churches throughout Wake County

First Board of Directors (established 1994):
Anna Neal Blanchard, Suzanne Chandler, Eva Clinding Tucker, George Deloache, Steve Derthick, Tommy Fonville, Betty High, Helen and Freddy Johnson, Horace Mason, Charlotte Pickett, Bill Prewitt, Kelvin Redmond, Delores Steele Richardson, Paula Rinehart, Hardin Sigmon, Carol Sloan, Vincent Terry, Bob and Maggie Wynne (with gratitude to all Board Members that followed)

Capital Improvement Campaign Committee:
Anna Neal Blanchard, Tommy Drake, Tommy Fonville, Kelly King, Johnny Morisey, Bill Prewitt, Carol Sloan, Delores Steele Richardson, Bob Wynne

Building for Hope Board:
Tommy Fonville, Freddy Johnson, Craig Herb, Johnny Morisey, Jay Silver

Endnotes

[1] From *Kitchen Table Wisdom* by Rachel Remen

[2] From *Daybreaks* by Paula D'Arcy

[3] Not until the 1990s did I finally begin to come to grips with what it meant to be the adult child of an alcoholic. This journey from trauma to healing was made under the gentle guidance of a counselor. I came to understand that alcoholism is a disease, and my feelings toward my father began to rework themselves. Negative images of my father that I'd held from my childhood through to adulthood gradually transformed into more positive memories. Happy times came back to me. I remembered how, upon being crowned Queen of Hearts during my senior year at Broughton High School, I had looked around to discover my father standing backstage, his arms laden with red roses, a soft smile of love for me on his face. I recalled how he loved his grandkids, often making evening visits to our house to watch Archie Bunker on television, bringing popcorn and M&Ms and whatever else the three children ordered by phone each night. He had a loving soul, and he did the best he could as he fought the disease that burdened him. He was a good father.

[4] From *Freedom of Simplicity* by Richard Foster

[5] From *Waking Up to This Day: Seeing the Beauty Right Before Us* by Paula D'Arcy

[6] From *Labyrinths: Walking Toward the Center* by Gernot Candolini

[7] From *Sacred Threshold: Crossing the Inner Barrier to a Deeper Love* by Paula D'Arcy

[8] Though our relationship with Ebenezer Mission and Pastor Gabriel was broken, Freddy and I continued to support other Haitian leaders with whom we had developed relationships as they provided nutrition, healthcare, education, and spiritual teaching to people in need. We continued to travel to Haiti with Hearts and Hands for Haiti with mixed groups from our community and the city of Raleigh.

[9] From *More Than Equals: Racial Healing for the Sake of the Gospel* by Spencer Perkins and Chris Rice

[10] "In the 1993 book *More Than Equals: Racial Healing for the Sake of the Gospel* by Spencer Perkins and Chris Rice, which I still use as a primer for understanding racial healing today, the authors mention that we must do three things if we are ever to get to racial reconciliation. First, we must ADMIT that the race problem still exists and that we have not crossed the racial lines that have divided us. It is still alive and well and so far has weakened the credibility of our gospel. Oh, how this must break God's heart. SUBMIT is step 2. We have to be honest before God and admit we cannot do this without Him, and we need His Spirit to guide us to this step. Only then can we ever submit to one another and begin to address the hurts between us. Lastly, we

must COMMIT ourselves to this ministry. It must become a lifestyle of loving the neighbor who is unlike us, in different skin than ours, with backgrounds unlike ours. We have to 'live it out.' It's not easy but it's possible, or the God of love would never have required it of us. The world is waiting to *see* a Christian and not just *hear* about one. It has taken about a year for the small groups I work with to really take this book to heart, and it leaves nothing out. It has broken hearts and created a willingness to follow the steps to reconciliation." –Reggie Edwards

[11] From *Tattoos on the Heart: The Power of Boundless Compassion* by Fr. Gregory Boyle

[12] From *Reconciling All Things: A Christian Vision for Justice, Peace and Healing* by Chris Rice and Emmanuel Katongole

[13] Today, Dr. Delores Steele Richardson is Director of the Greater Pleasant Grove Development Corporation, which provides a continuum of support for East Wake families.

[14] Linda's call was working with children and their parents in multiple programs at BTM. She received her Bachelor of Science Degree with a major in Social Work from Meredith College. She is now employed by North Carolina State University as a clinical research assistant.

[15] Stan Wiebe served BTM in many capacities. Today he is the founder and director of Hearts and Hands for Haiti.

[16] Reggie Edwards wore many hats. In 2008, the Independent News gave her the Citizen Award for Women of Color. She received the MLK Award/Making A Difference in Wake County from AARP; she received The News and Observer MLK Award for People Living the Legacy. Today she is the founder and Chief Encouraging Officer of The Encouraging Place in Raleigh.

[17] Though our ties to Ebenezer Mission had ended, we supported the leaders we had met there who had left to begin their own work. Pere, Chrismond, John François, and Jeremiah all had servant hearts and were committed to helping their Haitian brothers and sisters.

[18] From *My Utmost for His Highest* by Oswald Chambers

[19] From *Gift of the Red Bird* by Paula D'Arcy

[20] The ownership and leadership of BTM was transferred to Mount Peace Baptist Church. Our passion for racial healing and bringing awareness to others of our neighbors on the margins remained primary in our hearts. We supported the ongoing efforts of Stan Wiebe (Hearts and Hands for Haiti), by leading spiritual journeys to Haiti, and of Reggie Edwards (The Encouraging Place), by promoting racial reconciliation events.

[21] From *Help, Thanks, Wow: The Three Essential Prayers* by Anne Lamott

[22] From *Gift of the Red Bird* by Paula D'Arcy

[23] From *The Valley of Vision: A Collection of Puritan Prayers & Devotions*

[24] From the program at Freddy's Celebration of Life:

VISION STATEMENT
Praise God by fully utilizing my God-given gifts and talents to fulfill His purpose in creating me.
"Bring glory to God by doing the work He gave me to do."

MISSION STATEMENT
My mission is to help transform the abundant latent gifts and talents
stored up in the low-resourced community into active energy, propelling the Kingdom of God.

GOALS
Be a bridge-builder between needs and resources.
Be active in minority leadership development (i.e. story of Stephen)
Become more cross-culturally aware and sensitive

DEFINITION OF SUCCESS
"To **know** and **do** God's will."
"God measures our success not by what we have, but by what we **do** with what we have.

[25] From *Carry On: Reflections for a New Generation* by John Lewis

[26] From *Seeking with All My Heart* by Paula D'Arcy

[27] From a sermon by Rev. David Beam, Hayes Barton United Methodist Church, Raleigh, NC, November 27, 2022

[28] From *Turn My Mourning into Dancing: Finding Hope in Hard Times* by Henri Nouwen

[29] The following organizations represent hundreds of God's children who will benefit from God's multiplied provision: Seasons Village (partnering with single moms and their children to foster a strong foundation for intergenerational prosperity); Neighbor to Neighbor (cultivating life-giving mentoring relationships that result in communities of hope, justice, and compassion); East Wake Leadership Academy (a K-12 afterschool program that provides homework help, academic skill-building, leadership training, recreation, and youth employment); Southeast Raleigh YMCA (a cradle-to-career pipeline of services and interventions to support the children and families of Southeast Raleigh); Camp Sea Gull (building character in a nurturing environment that fosters self-confidence, independence, and respect for others); Triangle FCA (presenting to coaches and athletes, and all whom they influence, the challenge and adventure of receiving Jesus Christ as savior and Lord, serving Him in their relationships and in the fellowship of the church); Greater Pleasant Grove Development Corporation (serving as a partner for educational, economic, and community development, and as a catalyst for civic and personal responsibility among the residents of Wake County and the surrounding area); Your CenterPeace (proactively strengthening marriages and families); Note in the Pocket (providing quality clothing to homeless and impoverished children and families, with dignity and love); Hope Reins (pairing kids in crisis with rescued horses to find hope and healing); The Green Chair Project (repurposing donated furnishings for people facing the challenges of homelessness, crisis, or disaster); ROAR (dismantling systems of racial advantage and oppression through education, analysis, healing, community building, and institutional transformation, and seeking to restore

collective economic power and ownership to People of Color by reversing the historical impacts of white affirmative action); PAVE (providing support, training, information, and resources to empower and give voice to individuals, youth, and families impacted by disabilities); Growing Together Preschool (providing free early childhood education for low-income three- and four-year-olds for kindergarten success); Young Life (introducing adolescents to Jesus Christ and helping them grow in their faith); The Encouraging Place (promoting and inspiring an end to racism; encouraging racial healing and understanding to create equity within our communities); Hearts and Hands for Haiti (promoting the dignity of Haitians by coming alongside to share the love of Christ, contributing to their spiritual, educational, physical, emotional, and vocational development); Raleigh Mennonite Church (a community growing as disciples of Jesus, the Christ; in community we seek justice, healing, hope, and peace for all people); Focus Raleigh (providing a place for students to explore the real questions in life without judgment or expectation).

[30] Latesha Greene now has a B.A. in social work from Shaw University and an associate degree in applied science from Wake Technical Community College. Latesha is married, and she and her husband share five children and three grandchildren. She worked for Wake County Public Schools as a special education teacher for 15 years and is currently working as an exceptional resource teacher in Johnston County. "My passion is that every individual has an equitable opportunity to be successful—in the classroom and in real life. I'm a voice for the voiceless and a leader for the common good."

References

Bennett, Arthur, ed. *The Valley of Vision: A Collection of Puritan Prayers & Devotions.* Edinburgh: The Banner of Truth Trust, 1975.

Boyle, Gregory. *Tattoos on the Heart: The Power of Boundless Compassion.* New York: Free Press, 2011.

Candolini, Gernot. *Labyrinths: Walking Toward the Center.* New York: Crossroad, 2003.

Chambers, Oswald. *My Utmost for His Highest.* Uhrichsville, Ohio: Barbour, 1963.

D'Arcy, Paula. *Daybreaks: Daily Reflections for Lent and Easter.* Liguori, Missouri: Liguori, 2009.

D'Arcy, Paula. *Gift of the Red Bird: The Story of a Divine Encounter.* New York: Crossroad, 2001.

D'Arcy, Paula. *Sacred Threshold: Crossing the Inner Barrier to a Deeper Love.* New York: Crossroad, 2004.

D'Arcy, Paula. *Seeking with All My Heart: Encountering God's Presence Today.* New York: Crossroad, 2003.

D'Arcy, Paula. *Waking Up to This Day: Seeing the Beauty Right Before Us.* Ossining, New York: Orbis, 2009.

Foster, Richard. *Freedom of Simplicity.* San Francisco: HarperCollins, 1981.

Hawkins, Pamela. *The Awkward Season: Prayers for Lent.* Nashville: Upper Room Books, 2009.

Katongole, Emmanuel and Chris Rice. *Reconciling All Things: A Christian Vision for Justice, Peace and Healing.* Westmont, Illinois: InterVarsity, 2008.

Lamott, Anne. *Help, Thanks, Wow: The Three Essential Prayers.* New York: Riverhead, 2012.

Lewis, John. *Carry On: Reflections for a New Generation.* New York: Grand Central Publishing, 2021.

Lupton, Robert. *Theirs Is the Kingdom: Celebrating the Gospel in Urban America.* San Francisco: HarperCollins, 1989.

McIntosh, Peggy. "White Privilege: Unpacking the Invisible Knapsack." *Peace and Freedom Magazine*, July/August 1989, 10–12.

Nouwen, Henri. *Turn My Mourning into Dancing: Finding Hope in Hard Times.* Nashville: Thomas Nelson, 2001.

Perkins, Spencer and Chris Rice. *More Than Equals: Racial Healing for the Sake of the Gospel.* Westmont, Illinois: InterVarsity, 2000.

Remen, Rachel. *Kitchen Table Wisdom: Stories that Heal.* New York: Riverhead, 2006.

Made in the USA
Columbia, SC
10 August 2024

40238557R00136